Mining For Gold

Facilitation Skills to Unearth a Wealth of Ideas from Your Team

Mining For Gold

Facilitation Skills to Unearth
a Wealth of Ideas from Your Team

Michael A. Podolinsky

Singapore   London   New York   Toronto   Sydney   Tokyo   Madrid
Mexico City   Munich   Paris   Capetown   Hong Kong   Montreal

Published in 2004 by
Prentice Hall
Pearson Education South Asia Pte Ltd
23/25 First Lok Yang Road, Jurong
Singapore 629733

Pearson Education offices in Asia: *Bangkok, Beijing, Hong Kong, Jakarta, Kuala Lumpur, Manila, New Delhi, Seoul, Singapore, Taipei, Tokyo, Shanghai*

Printed in Singapore

4   3   2   1
07   06   05   04

ISBN 981-244-686-9

National Library Board Singapore Cataloguing in Publication Data

Podolinsky, Michael A.
Mining for gold : facilitation skills to unearth a wealth of ideas from your team /
Michael A. Podolinsky. – Singapore : Prentice Hall, 2004.
p. cm.
    ISBN : 981-244-686-9

1. Group facilitation. 2. Group problem solving. 3. Teams in the workplace. I. Title.

HD66
658.4036 — dc21   SLS2003035187

Dedication

To my loving wife Sarnai
Her love and perpetual encouragement
empowered me to finish this book.
Her smile, gentle touch
and strong faith in God
help make my life a daily joy to live.
She facilitates in my heart
a greater commitment
to become the best person
I can be.

Contents

Foreword

I first met Michael Podolinsky in a seminar he conducted many years ago. He was enthusiastic, he was focused, he was eagerly working the room. He was, in the best sense of the word, Mining For Gold.

Michael knew success of his seminar that day would depend not only upon his energy and expertise (which are truly enormous) but also upon the interest, ideas and participation of his audience members. He did not wait to see if they would speak out. He did not stand aside hoping for participation. He did not wonder. He did not wait. He took out his full set of skills and tools and set about Mining For Gold - the kind of Gold that makes meetings work, teams perform, companies profitable, and customers happy.

Over the years I have known Michael to work with hundreds of companies and organizations in countless situations. Whether he is teaching trainers, motivating sales people, building strong teams and teamwork or helping companies become more positive and productive, Michael has a special "knack" for getting people involved. He gets them to open up, listen to each other, participate fully and share their best ideas. Often, results at the end are more than anyone could have imagined at the beginning.

How does Michael do it? How does he consistently dig into the deepest well of innovation, ideas and enthusiasm of the team? How does he go Mining For Gold... and find it?

Now you have the answer right here in your hands. In this truly ground-breaking book, Michael Podolinsky has taken a career's worth of insights, ideas, experience and expertise and made it completely accessible and practical for you. *Mining For Gold* has everything you need to make your meeting more successful, your team more productive, your company more profitable... and your own work a lot more fun.

Michael tells you what to do, and what to avoid. He tells you how to prepare, and how to debrief after a meeting is over. He gives you checklists, advice, tips... even a set of great cartoons to keep your spirits high! And he does it all in a short, tight, easy-to-use format that will make this book one of your very best business investments.

Enjoy this book. Read it now, put the ideas to use, then read it again in six months' time. You will find your own skills and results steadily improving. Every step of the way, meeting after meeting, year after year, you will find that *Mining For Gold* helps you reach a new level, accomplish your next objective, attain a higher level of achievement.

In every way, *Mining For Gold* brings you precious, practical and very positive results. You've got the right tools here in your hands. Now turn the page, and dig in!

Ron Kaufman
Bestselling author of *UP Your Service!*

Acknowledgments

We would like to acknowledge the members of the National Speakers Association of the USA, NSA Australia and the Asia Speakers Association for their help and support through this effort. They are great professionals who are willing to share and give support and guidance.

We would also like to specifically thank our endorsers, Harvey Mackay, Dato Lawrence Chan, Ronald Tan, Larry Wilson, Winston Marsh and Mano Sabnani who graciously lent their names and credibility to this work.

We want to give special thanks to friend, colleague and consummate professional Ron Kaufman for his eloquent foreword.

We also want to thank our friends at the Singapore Institute of Management for their assistance over the years in our facilitation programs. Without them, many of our programs would not have been as successful and this book would not have been as complete.

A special "Thank You" to our publisher for their hard work and dedication to "getting it right".

Finally, we would like to thank our hundreds of clients who have allowed us to help them "Mine For Gold" in their backyards. Obviously, without their support and willingness to call us in to help them, this would only have been an academic or theoretical exercise instead of a hands-on, real-world, practical work.

Introduction

"Hmm ... no problem boss!"

"You can handle this, can't you?"

The boss asks you to facilitate an upcoming meeting. "No problem," you respond, after all, you are the head of personnel, training, HR or some other non-involved group.

"What's the objective and who's attending?"

"We want to get engineering and sales to agree on the new prototype design. This would involve sales executives, design and electrical engineers and the heads of both production plants in Singapore and Malaysia. In addition, three of our key customers from China want to sit in. They say that if this doesn't work, they're going to pull out all of their orders. You can handle this, can't you?"

Three problems:

One, you know NOTHING about engineering, design or sales.

Two, everyone attending is senior to you in the company or in their own organization and the intimidation factor can be unbearable.

Three, if this doesn't work, it will probably cost you and a couple hundred of your colleagues their jobs.

"No problem boss!" you respond.

Why no problem? You know Mining For Gold™.

Mining For Gold™ is a proven method for being able to facilitate ANY meeting by taking control of the variables that usually cause division, a loss of "control" or personal frustration.

Mining For Gold™ gives you control by helping you to plan in advance for potential obstacles that may become roadblocks, obstacles that inevitably arise and successful conclusion of a meeting with the prospect of ongoing progress.

In addition, Mining For Gold™ will help you uncover a wealth of valuable ideas from your team. Just as the old saying goes, "Still waters run deep," some of the best ideas, those that would make your organization more profitable, are left dormant in the minds of the less vocal workforce. We never hear these ideas because we have approached the matter the wrong way: dominant employees tend to orchestrate or take over the meeting such that the quieter ones never get a chance or are too intimidated to share. Many times, we simply have never asked them to share. Mining For Gold™ will help you uncover and profit from these hidden ideas.

For Mining For Gold™ to work for you takes dedication: an awareness of the principles, practice of the techniques and a belief not only in the process, but also in yourself as a facilitator.

Fortunately, if you have picked up this book, it is an indication that you have everything it takes to be good at Mining For Gold™.

Now, how did we come to write *Mining For Gold*? Simple. Luck and Wisdom.

Luck and Wisdom are deceptive mistresses. They favor the old, but not all the old. They love the inventive, but not all invention. They reward the risk taker, but often bankrupt the risk taker too.

When Wisdom or Luck smile on us, they often take many forms. Sometimes they show us the long smile of continued success. At other times, they give us only a quick grin followed by a smirk or worse, a frown.

In writing *Mining For Gold*, 22 years of hard work just seemed to come together all at once. The topic was hot in our seminars. The market timing was right. The world's largest publisher, Pearson Education, appeared. And on top of that, our thought patterns and concepts seemed to gel "just right".

In addition, my family agreeing to move to Asia with me and the formation of the Asia Speakers Association all came together at the right time to make this book not only possible, but auspicious in both timing and content.

Our good friend and fellow trainer/facilitator, Peter Ng, had put us in touch with Pearson. The editor at that time showed no interest. Six months later, another good friend, Delphine Ang of The Partners (they promote our seminars in Malaysia), also put us in touch with Pearson, and this time, the NEW editor was excited about the project. Success was within reach!

If you are wondering what this has to do with Mining For Gold™, the answer is EVERYTHING! If you want to get great input from your team, you need to take some chances – the chance that it might not work, the chance that you might lose face, the chance that you might get what you ask only to find out it's not what you want, etc. That is the same process we went through in getting this book out to you.

If you want to hear from everyone and not let one person on the team dominate, you need to try a number of tactics. Again, that was our approach. We priced out this book to be self-published. We had several smaller publishing houses interested, we consulted with clients, friends and family and finally, by not giving up, we got the publisher of our choice to publish this book.

What I've been describing here to you is the "luck" component. It's like what my old karate instructor used to tell me, "Mike, you MAKE your own luck." He meant, if you work hard, don't sweat the failures and just keep fighting, eventually, your opponent gives up and you win. Hence, you are "lucky".

Yes, it was a lucky break to get this book published. After just 22 years of work, our program has become an overnight success.

The wisdom part was a tougher pill to swallow. I tried to learn, to think, to grow with the material, but the material was growing with me. When I started at this, there was no book to read, no course to take and no one to ask. Only after I had been conducting facilitation for over 15 years did a workshop appear through the National Speakers Association in Tempe, Arizona.

That workshop changed my life. Finally, I could sit and learn from highly successful, highly skilled facilitators who were doing what I was doing. Amazingly, three-fourths of what they taught me was "spot on". That is, three-fourths of what they told us we had to do was exactly what I had been doing and teaching.

Of the one-fourth that did not coincide with their teachings, half of what they shared, I'd realized I was doing "wrong" or that there was a better way to do it. The other half of that quarter, I totally disagreed with. Statements like "Let it take as long as it takes" or "You can't rush a work of art" seemed ludicrous at best.

If Picasso could scribble a few lines on a napkin to pay for a dinner or Rembrandt could make a single line less than a meter long and create "Bird In Flight", thus impressing the world for ages, art CAN be rushed and still be art.

Further, in business, Lady Luck tends to favor the FIRST to hit the market, not the "most perfect".

I saw a speaker once (sorry, forgot the name) who showed half a dozen mousetraps, all of which were vastly superior to the basic "snap" trap. I'd never seen or heard of any of them and neither had anyone in the audience. His point (real wisdom) was that the old saying "If you build a better mousetrap, the world will beat a path to your door" was a myth.

Likewise, the folks teaching and, unfortunately, the people believing that you can only get real quality answers over time are clinging to a myth. We've gotten some really great answers for our people in a really short period of time. In fact, sometimes the shorter, the better.

It took me a while to knock that idea which I had "learned" from these pros out of my head. It has nothing to do with how LONG you spend getting an answer. It has EVERYTHING to do with how effective you are at drawing out the answers. If it takes you a week to get an answer because people are not comfortable in sharing, then, it takes you a week. If you can get people comfortable in 10 minutes, relaxed and open in 30 and sharing in 40 minutes, maybe the great answer comes in 60 minutes to 2 hours. Hanging out for two weeks will not necessarily give you better answers or ideas. Why it took me 20 years to get this, I don't know. The funny thing was, I knew it when I started. It's just that I had heard the other argument every year of my life growing up and had bought into it. Now that I "get it" again, life is accelerating and we are on a faster and more exciting ride.

Mining For Gold™ will not just get you great information from your team, it will give you the best possible information in the shortest possible time. It will be your ticket to success by showing you how to extract that valuable ore in the shortest possible time. And with our world changing as fast as it is now, time IS money and your success DOES depend on how fast you can get that information.

Finally, there's no 400-page academic "War And Peace" approach to this subject. As Abraham Lincoln once apologized for writing a 2-page letter with "I'm sorry for writing you this 2-page letter. I didn't have enough time to write you using just one", we do not want to have to apologize to you. The points are short, quick and easy to understand. More importantly, they are easy to implement IF you are willing to give them a try. In about 100 pages, an hour to read, you can change your life and your career. Go for it. If you have any questions, comments or additions, please e-mail me at mike@michaelpodolinsky.com. I usually respond within 48 hours. Put "Mining For Gold™" in the subject line.

Best of luck and wisdom to you. May all your encounters with your team be "facilis" and may you unearth a wealth of ideas from your team.

Know Before You Go

If you are to become a master of Mining For Gold™, you'll need to know what to look for before going headlong into a bad situation.

There is an old story of a priest, a rabbi and a minister fishing together. The priest and the rabbi usually fish together but on this occasion they decided to invite the new minister along. After fishing a while, the priest excused himself, got out of their boat and walked to shore on the water to relieve himself. The minister was impressed. After returning, again walking out to their boat, the rabbi decided he needed to take a comfort break. He stepped out of the boat, walked on the water to the shore and returned a short while after. Finally, the minister, not to be outdone and needing to ease his discomfort, stepped out of the boat and SPLASH, down he went into the lake. The rabbi turned to the priest and said, "I guess we should have told him where the rocks were."

It is helpful for every person who facilitates a meeting to know "where the rocks are" in facilitation. "Rocks" come in the form of people, places and things. Let's examine how to best use them in Mining For Gold™.

People are the tools of facilitation. Without them, there would be no facilitation required or the need for a facilitator. Firstly, never be upset with them, but rather, see them as simply a means to an end. If you need to get two sides together to agree or to create something, understanding the people involved and what they want is essential.

Zig Ziglar once said: "To get what you want, you must help others get what they want."

Never is this truth more evident than in Mining For Gold™. It behooves the facilitator to take time PRIOR to the meeting to understand the nature of each individual participant, what he or she wants, his or her "agenda", likes and dislikes as well as how others perceive him or her, his or her personality traits, similarities and dissimilarities.

Ninety percent of your overall success is dependent upon the behind-the-scenes preparation prior to the start of the facilitation rather than upon what happens once it begins. To help guide you, look at these three essential areas.

What is the Personality Profile of Each Participant?

Does the person participate in everything but rarely offer new information or, even rarer, START something? Is the person people-oriented who enthusiastically starts projects, but is poor at following up and details? Does the person look only at the bottom line financial and background data from an analytical standpoint? Is the person predominately bossy, driving for success at all costs with little regard for people's feelings? Or is the person a blend of personality types and has the ability to fit in comfortably where needed? Actually *all* styles can be a boon to the facilitator as all behavior styles benefit the process. However, knowing which is which and who might sabotage your efforts is essential. A good Miner of Gold™ strives to use each trait for the benefit of the meeting.

There are four basic behavioral styles and a fifth that is a blend of all four. None of these is right or wrong, they just tend to operate in different ways. We need to think about our style and the style of the person or persons we are facilitating in this meeting to know what compromises to make and how best to deal with them.

The four styles are the Accountant, the Boss, the Assistant and the Salesperson. The fifth is a blend of all four types.

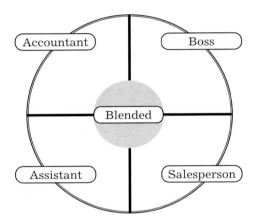

First, the *Accountant* types will tend to slow the process in favor of planning for success rather than jumping into ill-conceived plans. They help by giving structure and seeing possible pitfalls. Their knowledge in finance or planning can help a team get off to a positive and profitable start. They can also sabotage the process by slowing it so much so that key opportunities are missed.

Second, *Bosses* tend to push people forward to accomplish goals, often with little regard for those people. They are great at accomplishing a lot of work yet sometimes lose the support of the people they need to rely on. Their bottom line orientation and task-focused approach make them both a valuable asset and a potential input-killer.

Third, *Salespersons* love people, love getting things started, but you cannot always count on them for much follow-up or follow-through. They usually are instigators, not detail watchers. They inject a lot of motivation, enthusiasm and ideas to a group, but when the action steps need to be taken, they may be off on other "urgent" matters.

Fourth, *Assistants* usually do whatever is asked of them until they are overworked. Assistants rarely know how to handle all they have committed to do and often make commitments they cannot handle alone. Know what they already have on their plate before relying upon their follow-up.

Finally, the *Blended* type is a perfect mixture of all four. (I've never met one, but I've been told that they exist.) Actually, becoming a Blended type can be the goal of every Miner For Gold™.

Personally, as a Salesperson type, it took years of working with my Certified Public Accountant (CPA) and a consultant once a week for me to start thinking more analytically, planning our business growth, like an accountant.

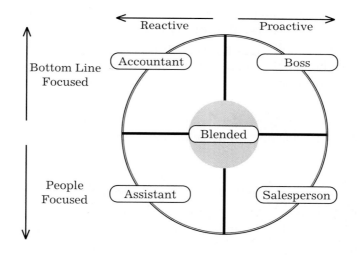

You will find the people in the top half of the Behavioral Styles model as being task, bottom line or activity focused. These people tend to be less empathetic to human issues and instead, focus on hardline issues like costs, profits, reaching goals and "success". They do not usually care as much about people and people's feelings. They are not wrong, it's just their make-up and focus. A good Miner For Gold™ needs to remember this when working with them and protect those who will need protecting.

Those on the bottom half are people focused. They have a tendency not to care about profits and results nearly as much as building relationships, being popular and accepted and having people feel good about themselves, the organization and the person in question. They are not wrong either, they just have a different set of priorities. A good Miner For Gold™ needs to be aware that these folks can make an organization go broke but are also good allies in protecting people and their feelings.

Those on the right side of the diagram tend to be proactive and initiate projects, plans and get things started. Use these folks to get your teams going or to start new lines of thinking.

The people on the left side of the diagram tend to be reactive and may need a little more prodding to get them off the starting line. They can also be wonderful at helping to put the brakes on a runaway horse or to give your team a better plan to follow or the person(s) to help follow up.

There is no hard and fast rule as to determining which person matches which personality type. Personal conversations, DISC™ tests, Myers Briggs™ tests, Personalysis™ tests, Neuro Linguistic Programming (NLP) training and so forth, can help give you an accurate picture of the people you are or will be working with. This, together with astute observations, can go a long way to preparing yourself for what lies ahead.

Don't come unglued if you mess up and misjudge people at first. Remember, there is no substitute for experience.

What are You Really Being Asked to Do?

More often than not, when we are asked to accomplish a goal, there is some kind of hidden agenda. The boss is using you to prove his team won't respond or work together. The client has already made up their mind and is only justifying their position. The decision is already made and you are merely there to "prove" the decision was right.

While you may be okay with this facilitation, future success may be jeopardized if participants find out there was an ulterior motive. Your future position of trust and strength may be permanently compromised. Make sure you know *exactly* what your mandate is and ensure your success by getting everyone, from management to front line, to agree with the decision of the whole group. Also, make sure that the information you mine successfully from your team has a definite purpose and use for the greater good of the team. You sabotage future facilitations if the group makes recommendations that will never be used or even looked at seriously. Not understanding this and walking into a facilitation blindly can greatly jeopardize your future successes.

What is the Group's Strengths and Weaknesses?

Doing a "SWOT" analysis on yourself and the group you are facilitating can make or break its success. SWOT is an acronym for Strengths, Weaknesses, Opportunities and Threats.

Find you and your team's *strengths* and *weaknesses*. As Leo Hauser, author of *5 Steps to Success*, has taught me, it is far more important to work on your strengths than to try to fix your weaknesses.

Strengths are those traits we possess that help us in life. Think of your strengths with people (outgoing, good listener, friendly, affable, affectionate, sincere, etc.), projects (good coordinator, systematic, dependable, logical, etc.), in business (money sense, ability to think of several things at once, etc.), creativity (in writing, verbally, planning, etc.) and personal strengths (contacts, friendships, fashion sense, timing, rhythm, faith, etc.).

In making a list of your strengths, try to make your list as comprehensive as possible. If you get stuck, ask some loved ones and close friends. I'm sure they will help you expand the list. You may want to consult a total stranger. It's amazing how those closest to us often overlook and even take for granted the jewels we wear so well.

Weaknesses are the traits we possess that hurt us in life. When listing your weaknesses, don't just list the obvious like "lack of education", "lack of a language skill" or "no contacts in business". Think more deeply and list those weaknesses that hurt us in more subtle ways like "skills haven't been updated in the last six months" or "haven't worked out in years and lack energy".

Try to make your two lists as balanced as possible. If you have a lot more weaknesses than strengths, you may also have a low self-esteem. If you have a lot more strengths than weaknesses, maybe you view your world through rose-colored glasses. Just ask your spouse or a work colleague to point out your real weaknesses. They are usually more than happy to do that for us for some reason!

Now, think of your top three weaknesses now, I'd gamble you've had at least two of the three weaknesses most of your life. Face it, if you've not fixed your weaknesses by now, what are the odds of you ever fixing them?

Likewise, it is good to know what your group's weaknesses are, but more importantly, how can you capitalize upon their strengths to get them to shift in favor of a compromise or towards your group's ultimate goal? Chances are, there are many great opportunities for you to take advantage of, if you are only willing to observe, listen and act upon their strengths while down-playing their weaknesses.

Opportunities are equally important to list. They provide direction and motivation. What are the opportunities in this group for you? Advancement? Increased power and prestige? What are the opportunities for your group and each member of the group? If you know them, you can use them as motivators.

Threats are important to consider as well. What can you, your team or individual team members lose if they are unsuccessful? What can they lose if they ARE successful? If we understand potential losses, we can control them better, troubleshoot and allay the fears of individual team members. A confident team will allow mining operations to begin.

Five Information Mining Tools to Get People to Open Up

"Five steps make it a lot easier."

The second key of Mining For Gold™ is to cover the Five Information Mining Tools™ that will get people to open up. Even the quietest of groups or individuals will share if you apply these five magic steps.

1. Set the essential ground rules of Mining For Gold™.
2. Systematize™ for input.
3. Use the ADA model to motivate attendees.
4. Take advantage of Proximics and Kinesics.
5. Always let them answer their own questions.

To understand how to apply and use the Five Information Mining Tools™, let's unearth them one at a time.

Mining Tool #1

Set some ground rules up front. You will find your facilitation days long, hard and tiring unless you set down some ground rules for participation first. After hundreds of facilitations and trainings, we've discovered four essential ground rules that will set the proper pace and support for a successful facilitation.

Ground Rule #1 – Your Role

The first Mining For Gold™ ground rule is to share with them *your role*. Unless you tell them what your role is, what you are willing or not willing to do, what you know, what you do NOT know and what you are capable of doing or not doing, they will assume or expect more than you are willing or able to deliver.

In addition, if you inform them that you are their "facilitation leader", they will expect you, the leader, to take charge. Once you have explained that you are only there for the process and not to add content, it's the start of a potentially successful facilitation.

If you are in a position that requires you to not only facilitate but add content too (a dual role), letting them know that is helpful too. If that IS your role, we strongly suggest that you set ground rules for yourself, that you contribute ONLY after everyone else has had a chance to share and then let them know you are stepping out of your role as facilitator and into the role of participant. Saying something like "Let me take off my 'facilitator's hat' and put on my 'team member hat' for a moment" will help your transition from facilitator to participant. Adhering to your own ground rules here will help you get buy-in and understanding from those participating.

If you do NOT list your role first or if you break your role or ground rules set for yourself, you'll find that the group will follow suit and you'll end up with chaos instead of a smoothly run facilitation.

Ground Rule #2 – Their Role

The second ground rule is to state *their role*. If they know what they are expected to do, chances are they'll do it. They may argue, debate or challenge it, but if you can finally settle into agreement with them on their role, you'll have a predisposition for facilitation success.

Anticipating participant problems and including solutions in this ground rule avoid a ton of problems later altogether. A typical participant's role will include elements like (but not limited to):

1. "Can we agree that we won't interrupt one another?"
   (get agreement)
2. "Can we all agree we will work cooperatively and build on each other's contributions?"
   (get agreement)
3. "Can we agree we won't digress and will remain focused upon the specific task/issue at hand?"
   (get agreement)
4. "Can we agree that each of us here MUST play an active role in this facilitation and each person will share to the best of his/her ability?"
   (get agreement)
5. "Can we agree that for the purpose of this task force, we will not look at rank or standing of all individuals present but rather consider the content of what is shared?"
   (get agreement)
6. "Can we agree to limit comments to two minutes or less and that no one should dominate the discussions?"
   (get agreement)

For as many problems as can be anticipated from your group, taking five minutes up front to set their roles will save you heaps of problems (and time) during the process and shore up the mine for extracting tons of valuable information gold.

Ground Rule #3 – The Goal

The third ground rule of Mining For Gold™ is to share the vision or *the goal* we are striving to achieve. If the goal is clearly stated and the group buys into it as their objective, the process becomes a lot easier.

First, they will all know what to work towards. Second, if everyone has the same idea of what the group is about, what they are trying to accomplish and where they are going, they will automatically pull together for the successful completion of that goal.

A perfect example came after the tragedy of 9-11. Not since World War II had the United States seen such unity between Republicans and Democrats, between the Senate and Congress. The elimination of the terrorists who attacked America became the #1 job for the country and the #1 priority of the nation. All other problems plaguing the country seemed to fall away and pale by comparison. Likewise, the SARS epidemic in Asia galvanized friends and foes alike to stop its spread across borders and within each country.

Mining in the right direction and at the right depth makes a big difference in motivation and commitment from the "miners." If you are able to fine-tune your group to agree that their task and mandate has meaning and significance, that it will serve them or their team if done properly and promptly, you will get results. Face it, if the group can't even agree on the goal of the meeting, it is pointless to continue beyond this juncture. A clear goal, however, sets a predisposition to its successful attainment.

Ground Rule #4 – Time

The fourth ground rule relates to *time*. Every aspect of time must be controlled: from the total time allotted to the facilitation to the time limit allocated for discussion of points; from the posting of times on a whiteboard, ripchart™ paper or chalkboard to the person responsible for keeping time (hopefully not you), etc.

Many professional facilitators believe you can't set time limits because you can't predict how long the process will take. Sorry folks, the reason they can't predict how long it will take is because they don't set time limits.

At Podolinsky International Pte Ltd, we build our consultancy on all aspects of developing people, time management being one of the essential tools of people development. If you've taken any time management training, you will probably remember C. K. Parkinson and what is known as Parkinson's Law: "Every task expands to the time allotted to it."

If you do not set time limits for a meeting, that meeting will take forever. If you set tight time limits, it will usually gel within those time limits.

Have you ever baked a chicken in an oven? An average chicken in an average oven takes about an hour. If you bake the same chicken in a pressure cooker, it takes about ten minutes. Why? Pressure! If you have a little real or artificially imposed pressure on the group you are facilitating, you'll "cook up" a solution a lot faster, and many times a better one than if you let every aspect of every idea be bled to death by endless discussions.

A corollary to Parkinson's Law is Podolinsky's First Law of Time Management for Facilitators and Trainers: "Every task will get done in the time allotted to it IF it's in writing, committed to by all relevant parties and involves more than one person in monitoring that commitment."

Assign a break timer, who not only watches for breaks but also discussion times, breakout times, and VERY important mile markers. Mile markers are warnings on time left for discussions, activities and the entire meeting. They might include: "one quarter done", "half way completed", "three quarters", "20 minutes left", "five minutes left", "two-minute warning", etc. Without mile markers, you'll always find you've "run out of time" with only a cursory glance at your topic. Mile markers keep the pressure on and get people to focus on the topic at hand, unearthing more ideas and getting a compromise in less time.

Mining Tool #2

The second tool for digging up group participation and thus golden ideas is to Systematize™ their input. Many participants are hesitant to speak up at any kind of public gathering. The larger the group, the more severe this hesitancy becomes. This fear of public speaking usually kicks in if there are more than four or five people in a group or if someone of greater power or authority is in the group (fear of authority). For some, the fear persists if they are with their peer group and want to fit in, be accepted and don't want to appear foolish in any way in front of their peers. Over the years, we have found that many middle managers fall into this category.

To help your group overcome this fear of speaking in public and the fear of speaking in front of peers or people of authority, follow the Mining For Gold™ secret and "SYSTEMATIZE™". This four-phase methodology will enable you to get anyone to open up at any time. In over 22 years of facilitating meetings of all sizes and in all industries, this technique has never failed.

Here are the four phases.

Systematize™ Phase 1 – Put it in Writing

Ask the group to write down what you want them to share or talk about. Getting them to write their thoughts down is a very non-threatening exercise.

Because it is non-threatening, people will be willing to take the action of writing their thoughts down (instead of staring at their shoes or the ceiling). By getting them to take action, they are now involved. Involved people eventually contribute.

Suggestion: Get them to write down *three things* instead of one. If you ask people for one thing, they often don't know what to write. They think, "Hmmm…what would be the best or most important?" This paralyzes their thinking. If you ask them to write down three things, they usually think: "Well, I'm not sure which is the best, but I've got to write three so I'll write the ones that come to mind first." As a result, you usually get three, often four, five or even six things.

Systematize™ Phase 2 – Share with a Partner

Have them share what they wrote down with one other partner, creating a dyad or discussion between two people. Even the shyest of people rarely have much trouble talking to just one other person.

If they are hesitant to share with the other person, perhaps because the latter has a standing in the organization way above theirs, the fact that they only have to read what they've written down makes their job easier and relatively stress-free.

In the process of sharing, they gain practice and confidence in expressing their ideas and opinions. They may even receive some acknowledgment or validation for their ideas.

Quite often, they find commonality of opinion that affirms their thinking and affords them greater confidence. A confident participant often becomes just that, a participant.

Systematize™ Phase 3 – Share in Small Groups

Have them share their idea(s) within a small group so that they get a chance to practice expressing their ideas and speaking in front of others. They may even garner some tacit acceptance of their concepts, encouraging them and bolstering their confidence.

Systematize™ Phase 4 – Share with the Entire Group

Now share what they have been writing and discussing with the entire group. At this phase, the information sharing is usually easy and free-flowing. They have in writing what they want to say, they have practiced saying it a couple of times and they know where they stand with colleagues. Let the sharing begin!

This phase 4 sharing can be done in a number of fashions:

1. You can literally go round the group one at a time and have people share one or more of their ideas.
   We suggest only one idea per person the first time round to encourage more people to share. If the first two or three people share all the unique ideas, it dampens enthusiasm and will discourage subsequent sharing.
2. You can ask for volunteers and have them share and discuss their points and gain the group's buy-in to the comments shared.
3. Have each partner share his or her partner's ideas. This not only gets the information put forth to the entire group, it can also promote team unity as each gets to "brag" about his or her partner's ideas. The one being bragged about tends to develop a bond or affinity for the one doing the bragging.
4. It's a good time for brainstorming or information "dumping" with some ground rules laid down at this time. Inform them that all ideas will be recorded and sorted or prioritized later. (See Chapter 6 for more ideas on brainstorming and creative mining techniques.)

Mining Tool #3

To get people to open up, apply the Attention, Desire, Action (ADA) model, an acronym we have shortened from the AIDA (Attention-Interest-Desire-Action) model used in many sales schools.

Attention!

In order to get them to "listen" and focus on a concept, you must first get their Attention. Attention can be captured through humor, games, props, magic tricks, startling statements, or quotes. These can be used to divert focus off themselves - their lives, hidden agendas and events of the day - and on to YOU or the PROCESS.

Some master facilitators would argue with this approach and insist that no facilitator should ever attract attention to him or herself. After all, the focus should be on the participants. True, but how can you get them to hone their attention on the task at hand when most participants go into meetings with a ton of emotional baggage, preconceived notions, thoughts, distractions, problems, side topics, etc.?

You must first take them out of their own mental world and back into the meeting with the group you are facilitating. We've had great success using these simple tricks or tools to garner and maintain attention.

Something as simple as telling a relevant joke helps them focus on you and the process. The one or two minutes invested in this endeavor may save hours later in re-explaining ground rules or having to return to the goal and redefining it.

So, first get their Attention, then get them working on the topic by focusing on themselves and the process.

Example #1

When working with a manufacturing group in Singapore in the early 1990s, we had a problem with one group who was always blaming another group. BOTH groups were hostile and not really willing to talk. They thought our program on team building was going to be just another one of management's "bright ideas".

To get their attention, we started by asking them to raise their hands if they were tired of getting blamed for the problems at their two plants. All raised their hands. Then we asked them who was professional enough to work on the solutions. Again, all raised their hands (hey... no option here). The last step was to get them all to answer a question in unison, "If you are not part of the solution, then you are part of the _____." They all shouted, "Problem!"

This got their attention and the rest of the facilitation and training went fairly smoothly. Six months later, when we conducted the second program for 2nd tier managers, it was a lot easier to get things going as they were already working towards one common goal.

Desire!

Once you have their attention off themselves, develop Desire (the "D" in ADA) in them to work on the goals laid out in the ground rules.

This is critical to a facilitator's success. Many wayward facilitators just assume that the participants have an automatic or natural Desire to achieve success. Such naiveté has killed many a facilitation effort.

To develop Desire, paint a picture of what they will gain from having it, how it will benefit them as individuals and collectively:

- Share with them some short-term benefits and the avoidance of short-term pain.
- Share any long-term benefits they may enjoy as a result of their successful participation.
- You may need a combination of carrots and sticks to ensure success with difficult facilitations.

Example #2

In working with a multilevel sales group in Malaysia, we opened with, "If there was a way for you to get people to see you as a friend instead of someone trying to 'sell' them something; and if everyone saw the need to have your health products; and if you converted 95 percent of the people you worked with into downline for you, would that be worth your while?" They shouted, "YES!"

Hey, that was one of the best pictures we've ever painted to get people to desire an outcome.

Action!

The last letter in ADA, another "A", is for Action. For any facilitation to be successful, the group will need to take Action.

- Who's going to do what?
- When will they accomplish it?
- How will they do it?
- Who will be informed?
- What are the ramifications to individual members if they don't do as they have agreed? (Use both the carrot and the stick here.)

With the ADA model, it is easier for any facilitation to work and for it to work within a tight timeframe.

Example #3

In Australia, we used the example of climbing Uluru (Ayers Rock) to get people to act. We shared. "I know that local Aboriginal people prefer that we do not climb Uluru because it is a sacred place where young men would go on a religious quest. Well, I too have been on a quest – as a man in my 40s – to stay young and to constantly stay in touch with my potential and to prevent myself 'getting old'. Likewise, I'd ask all of you not to just survive or exist for another day. Strive to climb to your highest peak of potential. Live your life like you are on a quet for excellence. Go forth and make a difference in your life by…"

The results were amazing and the call to action both emotional and highly effective.

Mining Tool #4

The facilitator may still have trouble with certain people either dominating the discussion or not opening up or contributing regularly. To counter both problems, the fourth magic step is to use *proximics* to get some people to open up and others to tone down.

Proximics influences the process depending on how close you are *in proximity* to the participants. The general rule of proximics is: The closer you are to someone, the less they'll talk. The further you are (within reason) away from them, the more they'll talk.

Culture plays a role in proximics. We need to be aware of this before we go any further. In North America, Singapore and Malaysia, if we stand one and a half arm's length from a person and shake hands, that's usually a comfortable distance for both parties. In some cultures, that would be way too close, particularly if the exchange is between a male and a female (Arab cultures). In other cultures like India or Sri Lanka, it wouldn't be close enough.

In any culture, what is comfortable proximics while standing may change when the parties are seated, but more particularly, when one is seated and the other is standing.

Here is where I have noticed that most facilitators drop the ball. While they would never even dream of invading someone's personal space by standing too close, they nonetheless get close to people when they are standing and the other person is sitting. It may still be the same one and a half arm's length away, but from the seated person's perspective, that is TOO CLOSE!

When we invade someone's personal space, we tend to shut them down as they feel self-conscious.

Many people who are not used to Mining For Gold™ tend to be in close proximity to a person when posing them a question. Aside from personal space being violated, all eyes in the room are now focused on that person. This "all eyes on them" effect further shuts them down.

Remember the problem we discussed earlier about the fear of speaking in public? When an entire group's attention is focused on someone who has this fear, his or her mind tends to go blank and he or she has a really tough time sharing and may not even remember his or her own name. Instead, use proximics to open them up. When you want someone to open up, do NOT walk over and look at him or her. This puts all eyes on that person and makes him or her reticent to share.

An expert gold miner will pose a leading question (to "prime the pump") from the opposite end of the room, and as the participant starts to share, the "miner" will glance over at someone else.

Most of the group will be looking at the facilitator OR the person the former is looking at, not the participant. Hence, you successfully take the pressure off the participant, allowing him or her to open up. You'll be pleasantly surprised at how taking the pressure off the person speaking can get him or her to open up and share his or her nuggets of wisdom with you and the team. This is a very simple "trick", but it really works.

How can you mine for gold if someone else is blocking the entrance to the mine?

Dominators usually block or inhibit others from sharing by preventing the hesitant speaker from getting a word in edgewise. If you successfully control the dominators in the group with proximics, you will open the door for the quieter participants to share their valuable input. The nice thing about using proximics to silence the dominators is that the group is not aware that you are silencing the nonstop talker. The less you are seen as an enforcer and the more you are seen as a facilitator or helper, the easier it will be to get *everyone* to trust you and open up.

Here's how you use proximics to silence the dominator. Just walking closer or sitting next to the person or persons who're dominating the discussion makes them feel a bit uncomfortable and this tends to quiet them down. Violating their personal space by getting near them (there is no need to look at them) usually makes them so aware of themselves and of the person who is doing this, they no longer focus on taking over discussions.

You don't have to sit in their laps! Just walk over and talk right next to them. Sometimes, if that is not enough, simply extending your hand onto the table or desktop of the dominator quiets them down.

In more extreme cases, walking behind them and placing a hand on their shoulders can work to achieve the same effect.

If it's a seated discussion, at a convenient time, for example, after tea break, change your seat so that you are seated next to the dominator.

If you have two people engaging in a lot of side discussions and distracting the group, after a break, sit between the two. This will hopefully encourage them to share with the team. If you are not the person with the most clout in the room, assign the seat between the two side talkers to the boss or person with the clout and allow that person's "proximics" to the two talkers to do the work.

Proximics can also be used in extreme cases when someone is breaking ground rules and not respecting others. If he or she persists even after a private word, consider really "getting in his or her face" and opening up his or her mind by finally breaking through the wall of insensitivity. (This is more easily done by an experienced miner for gold or someone with a higher level of self-esteem.)

Whether you use proximics to open someone up or shut someone down, it's a powerful tool in any facilitator's tool box.

Mining Tool #5

The final step to getting people to open up is to never answer their questions.

"An answer is the death of input."

Although you have set in the ground rules that your role is not to give answers but to facilitate, they may still forget and seek answers.

If someone asks, "What do you think?" or "What is the correct way to do this?" *Don't answer!*

If you do answer, you just put yourself in the position of "authority" and may get stuck in that role permanently.

Instead, use Mining For Gold™ "Tai Chi", that is, pass the question to either side of you, don't answer the question yourself. Rather, redirect the question back to the person asking it, or to the group at large by *you* asking a question such as:

"The reason you asked that question was...?"

"What do the rest of you think?"

"How do the rest of you feel about that?"

"How would you all handle this?"

"What do you believe to be the best way(s) to approach this question/idea/process?"

"Does any of you have an answer/opinion about...?"

"How has this been handled in the past?"

"Is there a policy in place to cover this?"

"How would the competition handle this?"

"What would we have done in the past?"

"If you picture yourself doing it, what would you imagine to be the outcome?"

Asking such questions helps you toss the ball back to the team you are facilitating ("tai chi") and keeps you from becoming the "authority" or central focus of the facilitation. The net result? High grade gold ore flowing from your mine.

Another alternative to answering questions directly is to first acknowledge the question with, "Thanks for that question. It's a good question." Then break the group into smaller discussion groups. The assignment or question(s) you give each group can vary with the situation and as gold miners, we are only limited by our own creativity.

If after throwing the question back to the group and no one feels comfortable answering, break them into groups of three to five with an assignment to come up with three possible answers to the question. Their answers have to fit into the following three categories:

First, how would we answer the question in an ideal world setting?

Second, how would the answer be, given the real world scenario?

Third, in a world that's ten times tougher than this world (one-tenth the budget, ten times the government restrictions, one-tenth the workforce available, etc.), how would the question be answered?

By doing this exercise, you are allowing them to discuss the issue in a less threatening environment. When they share their answers with the rest of the team, you'll have gotten a ton of great feedback and never have to answer the question!

These five Information Mining Tools™ for getting people to open up and share really work. We've mined some groups where we were told they NEVER open up and share. Yet, within a couple of hours of using the five Information Mining Tools™, there was a complete free flow of golden ideas and opportunities. Practice is the key to making the five Information Mining Tools™ work optimally for you.

chapter
3

Keeping It Light

Few facilitators understand the need for keeping meetings light. Many professors and other academics tend to think in terms of tactics, content and information-sharing instead of *results*. Chief executives generally think in terms of results instead of the PROCESS. Yet, the *process* is essential to obtaining desired *results* in Mining For Gold™.

If a meeting or facilitation is light, fun and easy-going, people relax. Relaxed participants are more likely to come up with new and creative solutions and ideas and are more likely to share. Anyone who is nervous, fearful, anxious, angry, hostile, bored or indifferent, will rarely, if ever, supply the gold miner with valuable nuggets of what the group needs.

The secret is to keep it fun, light and interesting while maintaining focus on the inevitable outcome.

Keeping it light maintains the group's energy and that will help the group accomplish its task(s) and achieve its goals and objectives.

Humor Them

Humor creates an etiolation in the brain, a predisposition to absorption of information. Research has also shown how humor creates an endorphin-rich environment in the brain. These naturally occurring chemicals enhance creativity and afford you quicker responses from attendees.

Still other research has shown how humor boosts the immune system, relaxes the individual and makes the person feel better about him or herself. That's why laughing clubs have formed all over India, moving to the rest of Asia and all over the world.

Here are a dozen ways to help you keep your next gold mining experience light.

1. YOU must be "in fun". Robert Henry, a great humorist, taught me in the early 1980s: "To be fun, you must STAY 'in fun'." He means that if you are too serious, come down hard on someone or lose your cool in any given situation, it will be very difficult to get that person, and usually the entire group, back into fun. Contrast someone who keeps things light with someone who DEMANDS success, DEMANDS answers, DEMANDS input from people. Would you respond well to such a person? I wouldn't and few people would.

2. Take a stretch break every 30 minutes. Tom Watson, the founder of IBM, once said, "The mind can only absorb what the seat can endure." Studies show that productivity takes a nosedive from the very start of the facilitation, and retention, listening, attitude and information flow take a dramatic dip after 30 minutes. Taking a 30-second stretch break every 30 minutes maintains energy, keeps people focused on tasks and often breaks stalemates on discussions.

   Don't worry about wasting time with these breaks. In eight hours of facilitation, they only take about four to five minutes of the group's valuable time. The positive results, however, can be quite dramatic.

CAUTION: Not all stretch breaks are created equal. Surprisingly, we found that stretch breaks need to be choreographed and planned. In using stretch breaks where everyone is left to his or her own devices to decide on the method of stretching, it is actually WORSE than if we do not take the stretch break at all. "Do your own thing" kind of stretching actually diminishes a group's energy.

It is far more productive to have everyone stretching together (Japanese style) just as everyone works together to achieve optimal performance. Further, it also helps to end with a laugh or some fun at the end of the 30-second stretch. Some ways to achieve this include:

- Working "faster" towards the end of a stretch (to the point they can't keep up, causing them to laugh).
- Asking them to do something they would obviously never do like turn to "punch" a neighbor. We have had groups do half a dozen karate punches in the air in front of them, after which we ask them to turn to the person next to them, implying that the next step is to start punching each other. This usually draws much laughter from the groups long before anyone throws a single punch.
- Having them unsuspectingly hold an awkward position like having them inhale and hold their breath. As they are forced to release their breath, 99 percent of the time they laugh. This laughter is the energy booster more than the exercise itself.

3. Use cartoons and humorous pictures to help make a point. Neuro Linguistic Programming (NLP) has taught us that at any time, 30 percent of the people in any group are in a visual-learning mode. If you use visuals, particularly with males, you will, more often than not, be able to elicit a laugh from them. (We find that men tend to move in and out of visual orientation more often than women.)

This laughter can be translated to results by creating an etiolation in the brain, that is, a predisposition to openness. (From a legal standpoint, just make sure you have copyright permission to use the picture or cartoon.)

4. Follow the energy of the group. When the energy drops, a Miner For Gold™ will take a formal break, put them into smaller

groups, add a prop, share a joke or insert some form of levity into the program. A close monitoring of energy can make a huge difference in the success of the facilitation.

5. Make fun of yourself. In 1982, I heard Bob Richards, an Olympic gold medalist, share that self-deprecating humor is the safest and most effective form of humor. After all, how in the world can someone say you offended him or her if the only one you made a joke out of was yourself? Fortunately, in my personal case, I was blessed with an abundance of raw material!

    As an example of how to use humor to encourage participation or overcome hurdles, imagine someone doesn't understand something and says something that is obviously off base and the group wants to turn on that person for being "stupid" or "foolish". Take the pressure off that person and bring the focus back to you. Say something along the lines of: "Forgive me, I think I must have set this up wrong. That's the first mistake I've ever made... (brief pause) again."

    An alternative would be: "Wow! Please forgive me for not making it clear what we are working on. I can see why you'd say that. Sometimes, I just open my mouth to change feet." (The implication is this – I put my foot in my mouth.) Another I've heard used is, "Sorry I wasn't clear on that. You see, I graduated in the third of the class that made the top two-thirds possible."

    Deploying such statements lightens the mood and eases the pressure off that person who misunderstood. By helping that person save face, you gain a friend and everyone else learns that you will protect him or her if he or she makes a mistake. That really helps to get people to open up.

    Coming up with some self-deprecating tag lines like that in advance will make it easy for people to make mistakes and not look foolish. The humor builds rapport within the group, relieves tension and enhances your position as their facilitator.

6. Use a prop to get them to laugh. There is something we teach in our Creative Training Skills program that applies here to facilitation. It's what we call meeting room inertia. Remember the laws of inertia from physics? A body at rest tends to stay at rest; a body in motion tends to stay in motion. Likewise, a meeting room (for training or facilitation purposes) develops

an inertia of its own. A quiet room will tend to stay quiet, a noisy room, noisy.

"If you want to mine some real gold, ya gotta make some noise!"

If you have a quiet group during the facilitation and no one is willing to offer ideas, using a prop to get them to laugh will add "noise" to the room. Generally, the ones who have something to share but are hesitant will now feel comfortable in sharing.

Example: If a group gets quiet and won't answer a question or share what their next step is, I'll brandish a meat cleaver (plastic) that's been hidden away and say, "We need some input here folks." This usually generates laughter and then someone inevitably shares what was on his or her mind. The laughter or "noise" overcomes their hesitancy to break the frosty silence by sharing.

NOTICE: Many professional facilitators would object to this and claim that we, as facilitators, should neither rush the process nor become the focus of the facilitation. They believe we need to let the process take as long as necessary. I disagree and find we get results (and often better results) ten times faster by getting people to laugh. It gets their creative juices flowing and better results for us and for our clients.

Another example of a prop is to take out a "discussion ball". Share with your group during the laying of the ground rules that if the group doesn't have anything to share, you'll take out the discussion ball and toss it to someone to share an idea like in brainstorming. No ideas are criticized, the ball is used just to get discussions going again.

For each person who catches the ball and shares one idea or option, no matter how silly, the group is to clap once for that person after which the ball is tossed to someone else and the process is repeated until there are ten options on the board.

7. Sweet rewards. Few people hate sweets. They may avoid them. They may not buy them. But few people refuse them. At the onset of Mining For Gold™, we toss sweets to the participants, thanking them for their input. Just like mercury tends to bring out gold in a sluice gate, sweets tend to bring out the golden ideas and input we desire.

Someone breaks the ice and shares an idea, he or she gets a Tootsie Roll™. Someone disagrees and shares a different point of view, he or she gets a Smartie™. Someone answers a direct question candidly (or should we say "candyly") and gets a mint. A participant shares something profound and gets a Kit Kat™. This exercise leads us to the conclusion that psychology has taught for years: What is rewarded (no matter how small the reward) will be repeated.

The longer the facilitation, the fewer rewards we hand out. This surprisingly doubles or triples responses. It's the principle of *variable reward*. Psychology has proven that variable rewards will get you more responses than fixed rewards. Try it!

Once the group is back to sharing and participating amongst themselves, we as facilitators stop, shut up and sit down. Mining For Gold™ is now at work. The sweets merely prime the pump to make the process fun enough to where it becomes self-rewarding. After that, intervention becomes a distraction so we avoid it.

In addition to sweets, we give out tokens like money (currency from foreign countries like Mongolia, Indonesia or Vietnam where the printed note is worth less than the Tootsie Roll™), plastic "smile" gifts, left-over sales incentives, books, tapes, CDs, plastic award medals, plastic trophies, quote books, rubbers (erasers for our friends in the Americas), etc. ANYTHING that is fun, useful or simply gets a laugh. Handing out gifts and sweets lightens the load for you as the miner and "magically" entices people to be more involved.

CAUTION: We toss them out to people to save time. Culturally, you may have to explain this and get their permission. Some "old school" people in Asia may be offended. We suggest you give them the option of being "handed" their reward.

8. Smile! People get about as serious as we allow them to get. If you are not "in fun" (in the spirit of fun) and HAVING fun, your group and the nature of the discussions will get "serious" and maybe maudlin. If your face and manner say this is fun, they will tend to be "in fun".

"But Michael, it's a serious subject like setting the budget."

And your point is? Nothing in this world, NOTHING is so serious that a little levity can't be brought into it. I love Irish wakes, they celebrate the person's passing into a "better world".

Layoffs? Damn serious. They need to be discussed with more humor than any other topic. In sharing with a YPO (Young Presidents Organization) chapter one day, one of the presidents said, "We don't call it cutbacks, we call it 'Saving for a rainy day'." She had it right.

Add a little fun to a discussion on cutbacks or layoffs with ax-falling jokes or quips, YOUR neck being chopped, funny stories shared by someone who was expected to be cut, etc.

If you need to remove a limb to save the body, such lines as "I didn't use that arm much anyway" can make the surgeon's job a lot easier.

YES, that sounds warped. Anyone with a heart would think the same. Still, I learned more about "acceptance" from children with cancer and contrite patients with terminal illnesses than I ever did from "normal" or "healthy" people. MOST have a wonderful sense of destiny and humor. I've also read countless stories of patients who joked with the surgeons and nurses and as a result, these said they worked twice as hard to save their "star" patient.

Don't we *ever* get serious? Are we expected to be clowns?

Of course we get serious. Being fun is just to start off Mining For Gold™ or to insert the energy back into the mining process.

Using a non-facilitation example, I once heard a telephone company spokesman address a crowd of very hostile tele-marketers in an after-dinner speech. Their phone rates had increased almost ten-fold in just one month's time. They were ready to roast this poor guy alive.

Instead of immediately trying to defend his company's position, the spokesman walked up to the lectern with his dinner napkin, folded it into a triangle, making a bandit's mask for himself. He pointed his finger like a gun and told them all to "stick 'em up!" They laughed.

The "robber" had come to call *looking* like a robber. He made a few comments then about being nervous about the rope behind the head table and how he liked his neck unstretched. You had to like the guy. As a result, everyone listened to him. Magic!

The point is, get the participants to focus on something positive with humor and then extract the golden nuggets as you lead them down the path of productive mining.

9. Let them get out early. How many of the people reading this want to really spend a lot more time at work? Darn few (except for the criminally insane). Likewise, most folks don't want to beleaguer the process. As a result, consider sharing, "As soon as we are done with this, we can all leave." Many times, that will give you quicker closure and can actually be a source of humor. (It sure changes some people's motivation to participate.)

   There are many ways of getting this message across.

   Example: "You all agreed, we would get out early if we completed the ten-step Plan Of Action (POA) before 4pm. Well, looks like we are staying until midnight as you have been discussing point #4 for the past hour. Just thought you'd like to be reminded." (This is said with a little sarcasm for humor's sake.)

   NOTICE: Some professional facilitators would TOTALLY disagree. "Let the process take as long as it takes!" they would cry. We disagree. Any fool can come up with a great answer in 99 years. A Miner For Gold™ can facilitate a similar answer 99 percent as good in 30 minutes to two hours. It is the combination of challenge, getting out early and occasional reminders that make this a "fun" technique to use in facilitation.

10. Games are by their very nature, FUN! When the participants get stuck or are in stalemate, get them involved in a brainstorming game or a game to draw them out.

    Example: Line up in two lines. Have the first person in one line share the #1 reason NOT to do something. The other line's first person shares the #1 reason TO DO it.

    Each person in each line shares his or her "reasons" alternately. All pros are recorded on one flip chart and the cons on another.

    Keeping them in the same groups, have them repeat the process but switch their assignments. In other words, the group that shared the reasons to NOT do something now has to share reasons TO DO it. But they cannot repeat the answers previously provided.

    The other group that previously shared what to do now shares the reasons NOT to do it. These are recorded as well.

The lists are compared and the group discusses their ideas. Fun. Silly. Productive.

Games are only limited by our creativity. In the reading list at the end of this book are several titles that list games for trainers and facilitators. In reality, you should also be able to come up with your own. Think "opposites", "groups", "ranks" (in the organization), "genders" for groupings and TV game shows, board games, kids' games, adult games, sports games for models to follow. YOU may be the next contributor to our "Games For Facilitators" book.

11. Play devil's advocate. When Mining For Gold™, playing devil's advocate and thus changing the rules of engagement can be a fun way to up the energy and flow of the discussion.

Instead of being polite, listening intently and keeping the focus on them and their ideas, you start to become a total contrarian.

This flies in the face of everything we've said so far, but that's the beauty of it. It is so off base it makes a stuck or lethargic group come alive.

If you doubt this, think of one of the most popular television shows of the first part of the millennium, The Weakest Link. It was just another "guess the answer" show but the hostess was so hostile and rude, people loved to hate her.

Tools you can use to make this effective include:

- Argue with them. Tell them how wrong they are and don't let them off easy with any idea they assert.
- Laugh at their ideas. Tell them how absurd their logic is.
- Put forth your own ridiculous ideas and assertions — the more wacky or far-out, the better.
- Take a very unpopular stance and then change your mind mid-stream, only to take up an even less popular option.
- Agree with the most popular opinion but for all the wrong reasons. (This will usually unveil hidden flaws.) For example, if someone's position is to increase staff pay by 20 percent, agree with him or her and say, "Yes, and each of us will work 20 percent more hours to earn it too!" or "Yes, and raise our targets and quotas 20 percent to pay for it!" or even, "Yes, and let's sell off our desks and computers to pay for it."

Have fun with it. That's part of its overall appeal.

Please bear in mind, at some stage you will have to let them know what you were doing. Once they know the technique, it may be more difficult to use it again with the same group.

12. The last method of adding "fun" or "humor" to the facilitation probably should have been the first. Make the facilitation productive. If people can see that THEIR ideas are being considered, THEIR ideas make a difference, THEIR ideas are listened to, analyzed and adapted for use, they will find the process FUN.

One of the great tragedies of life and certainly of Mining For Gold™ is when someone contributes and his or her idea (vital "soul" energy) is ignored. It happens more often than you think. Someone shares an idea and the average facilitator says, "Okay... any other ideas?" OUCH! Not only will that person not share in the future, everyone else in the group learns that sharing from your heart and soul gets you ignored or, in extreme cases, shot down in flames.

Statements that get you "out of fun" include:

- "That's not exactly what I was looking for..."
- "Maybe..."
- "Does anyone else feel the same way?"
- "Not that..."
- "Wrong!"
- "Perhaps, that is one way to view this..."
- "I'm not so sure..."

or simply

- "NO!"

Another common way inexperienced facilitators shut people down for sharing is simply ignoring them, their ideas or contributions.

As we had stated earlier and as psychology has proven, what is rewarded will be repeated. The flip side of the coin is: what is ignored *will* disappear.

Here we vehemently disagree with many of our facilitation counterparts. Some have told us that you NEVER acknowledge someone's contribution because to do so could be seen as bias.

Saying "thank you" to one and not the other gives the impression of approving one and rejecting the other. They believe in the "null hypothesis". They attempt to remain neutral and not show any emotion or reward any contribution from anyone.

In Mining For Gold™, the key is to reward PARTICIPAT-ION and not the CONTENT of the answer. Smile, nod, laugh, thank, toss a sweet or whatever it takes to reward the sharing.

Strive not to pass judgment on whether you think the idea or sharing has merit or not. That is for the group to decide. The essential element to always keep in mind is to be consistent.

True, you cannot be that consistent all the time. You will make mistakes. Face it, you would also make the same mistakes if you tried NOT to reward anyone. The unintentional smile, nod, lilt in your voice, added eye contact or some other nonverbal communication would give you away. Remember the old adage "you cannot *not* communicate". We find it much harder NOT to show reward to participants than it is to consistently reward everyone's participation.

By helping people feel they made a difference, they will be motivated to participate and find their participation "fun" and rewarding. It is as simple as: Benefit — they stay involved. No benefit — they withdraw.

Find a Way to Show Progress

"Almost there!"

H ow deep is the shaft? How many nuggets have been taken out of the mine so far? How close are we to the Mother Lode?

Once underway, any facilitation stands a good chance of stalling. Face it, even the best of groups with a high sense of purpose can stagnate.

When a group stalls, frustration sets in and people feel progress is impossible. Nothing can be further from the truth.

To get your group back on track again, one of the many "lubricants of progress" is to show the mining progress itself.

People get frustrated and feel stymied if they are not getting anywhere in life or in their work. By showing them what they have already accomplished, you free them from this mentality of "impossibility" and get them back on the track of "possibility".

Example: Make a "Wall of Progress" and show them as you go along, what they have successfully completed and how close they all are to achieving their previously agreed upon goal or objective. Update the wall as time goes on.

Another thought is to start with a "Mandate" and use it to let them know they are learning, making progress or finding solutions.

What's a "mandate"?

A mandate is a combination of tasks the group is given to accomplish in order to achieve a greater goal. When we refer to a mandate, we are talking about the specific points as posted on a wall or on a whiteboard that can be "ticked off" as they are accomplished.

In conducting public programs in Mining For Gold™, we often ask the group to share in smaller groups their top ten frustrations or problems in facilitation. As each small group comes up with their list, we combine them one-at-a-time from each list onto a master list, getting "buy-in" on each topic or point.

Recording these points on ripchart™ pages (five or six points to a page), we tack them adjacent to one another on a wall. (You should always rip off a page you have written on and tack or tape it to the wall. Never flip it over and lose the idea from view or from people's minds and memory.) Once all the problems or points have been recorded and posted, that becomes your mandate.

We put ourselves on the line by saying: "Okay, we promise to cover them. If we don't, ask for your money back!!!!". Participants now feel EMPOWERED to ensure that all points are really covered as promised. You too can do this by proclaiming: "We will come up with suitable solutions to all these issues *or* I'll personally wash all your cars for a week." (or some similar "torture").

As they offer suggestions to the problems listed, walk to the wall displaying their "mandate" and strike off each one as they are dealt with. It's the perfect way to make sure your gold mine produces a TON of valuable ideas.

Never put up anything on the mandate wall that you will not be able to cover. Occasionally, people do ask for help with problems that are not related to the subject we are facilitating. It could be a training, budget, power or ancillary issue. We tell them up front that that is not part of what we have time to cover, but we do offer them an alternative such as speaking to the facilitator at break time or over lunch and move on.

By doing this, you will never get stuck having to cover side issues or problems because these were addressed at the beginning. Would that make your next facilitation easier?

By the end of the session, hand the three, four or five sheets to the small groups and ask them to think of at least five solutions to each problem. They will always come up with at least one solution to each problem and sometimes five or six. Acknowledge their contributions, after which they will realize that they do, in fact, know the answers.

Other ways of highlighting the group's progress include:

- Asking them what they have accomplished so far.
- Making a new list of concepts or action steps they have agreed upon.
- Breaking them into smaller groups and have them report on what they have accomplished, achieved or learned up to that point.
- Having a contest amongst participants to come up with the ten most significant ideas the team has achieved up to that juncture.
- Systematizing™ the inputs of what they have accomplished by having them write down three things that have been accomplished, and sharing it with a partner, sharing with in a small group and then sharing with the group as a whole.

The main concept is to view the session in terms of PROGRESS instead of FAILURE. Remember, the only time we fail in Mining For Gold™ is if we QUIT or we FAIL TO TRY!

Focus on Solutions, Not on Problems

H ow to mine is a better focus than how hard it will be to mine. One of the great challenges for facilitators is keeping things positive. Many participants come to a facilitation NOT to look for solutions to their problems, but to complain about their problems.

Herein lies one of the great challenges for those mining for rich deposits of golden ideas; you must *listen* to their problems yet not *focus* on them. Keep the group focused on *solutions*.

This is similar to the problem faced by Tivia in the story, Fiddler On The Roof: How to keep from falling off the roof while continuing to play the fiddle.

Here are ten options that we've developed to help you magically keep the group focused on solutions and not on problems. We call them Solution Focused Options (SFOs) in Mining For Gold™.

Option One

This should be stated in the ground rules: that complaining or the presentation of new unrelated problems is not allowed during the meeting. So if any participant begins to side-track the discussion by complaining, gently remind him or her that that was not what you agreed to up front, adding, "Can we please get back to the solutions? Wouldn't you all agree?" (Get agreement.)

If you forget to set this ground rule up front or you assume you will not need to do so especially with a group you know well, you can add it as an additional ground rule by stating, "I was remiss when we got started and forgot to add one ground rule I always include in a session of this nature. Would it make sense to all of you if we limit our discussion to one issue until we have in place a reasonable set of solutions before we start bringing up other issues?" (Get agreement.)

"If that's the case, may we agree not to raise other problems until we've solved the one we are currently focusing on?" (Get agreement.)

If someone insists that the problem is related to the one that is already on the table, then getting a group consensus or even voting can help you direct the flow of the facilitation. No matter how the "voting" goes, adding the ground rule now may help you control the facilitation later on.

Option Two

Change the nature of the discussion. By shifting to a new method of gaining information, you can thwart someone who is constantly shifting to the negative by putting the group in a more structured facilitation.

Example: Try a small group discussion or brainstorming session by breaking your group into smaller subgroups of five, four, three or even pairs. The smaller the group, the less negative impact one complainer can have on the entire process.

By giving each group a different task (or even the same task) and then marrying the components together after 10, 20 or 30 minutes, you've effectively brought about progress for the groups that do not contain the complainer. And, if properly structured, even the group that contains the complainer, because of a tight focus and time limit, will be productive as well.

Another example is to have them individually write down three solutions to a problem you are working on. Put all the ideas up on a ripchart™ and then go through a process to get them to pick and choose the best options. It is the process that controls the negative person.

Option Three

Appoint the negative person as an assistant in a way that does not allow that person to control the conversation. These tasks would include:

- A scribe (with a TON to write down)
- Someone to catch nay sayers or rule breakers
- A secretary/recorder of "minutes" or ideas
- Any other job you can think of to keep him or her occupied

Some facilitation gurus might argue that this is manipulative and counter-productive to a well-oiled group and may hamper creativity by restricting someone who could very well contribute great ideas.

We agree and admit, "Guilty as charged." But this is where the facilitator Mining For Gold™ has to use a little common sense. It might take a developed gut feel to determine if this person is just complaining or has real issues that need addressing. This comes from a combination of sizing up group reactions and your own experience coupled with your mandate for the group.

Personally, if someone is distracting the group from the process, it's time to make a change. We (usually) don't have unlimited time and resources so we need to use them judiciously.

As far as it being manipulative is concerned, we call it diplomacy or just good gold mining skills. Think of it this way. If a child is bugging a parent with a ton of questions, getting the child to work on a project or play in the yard so that the parent can get something done, is that manipulation, diplomacy or just good parenting skills? We'll let you be the judge.

Option Four

Ask how the issue raised relates to the current task at hand. This works particularly well when there is no obvious connection. Usually the complainer backs off after he or she realizes his or her mistake. Sometimes they make the connection and you can pursue it without having turned that person off from the process.

Option Five

Try off-line comments to the complainer. Take a break when it happens or wait for a convenient time for a stretch or coffee break and talk to the difficult party at that time.

Many times, they are unaware of their behavior and simply talking about it and its disruptive effect can get them to stop. Tact is the key so the participant doesn't "go on strike".

On rare occasions, the individual may inform you of the reason behind his or her behavior - to do battle or to jockey for a fall back position. Talk it through. The problem usually gets fixed with an offer to protect his or her position until the issue gets thoroughly discussed.

The fear of many less experienced facilitators (particularly those of lower authority in the organization than the person they need to curb) is that it can be a bad move politically. They could be held accountable to that person long after the facilitation or put into "cold storage" in the company.

To these facilitators, our advice is - practice well ahead what you'll say if this situation arises. Put into your ground rules that your role may require speaking to someone off-line. Ask if the group is comfortable with that and get a unanimous decision.

If the need does arise to fix a problem off-line, ask more probing questions to get the person's input rather than sharing your own opinions. Try: "I've noticed a lot of complaints about a great many issues. Is there something I'm doing wrong in the process that makes you want to bring these up?" See what the person says. Chances are, he or she will say he or she was not aware of it. But by putting the burden of the problem on your shoulders in a way that obviously isn't your fault, he or she rarely if ever will have a problem with you.

If that person does have a problem with you, thank the person and ask for helpful suggestions and gradually work your way back to the mandate and have the group come up with a plan that will help you achieve the desired outcome.

By getting that person to understand that the group has to stay on track and that your way of facilitating really is working, you will have resolved the bulk of the problem(s).

Option Six

Take the entire topic off-line. If one of your topics is riddled with complaints about ancillary issues, leave the minefield for another session and return to Mining For Gold™.

You can do this immediately upon hearing a ton of complaints on a topic or leave it until after you have had a break.

Consider shifting the focus to brainstorm the problems one at a time in small groups or in pairs or triads (groups of three) as appropriate. The structure solves the interruptive or negative influence of one person and shifts the group back to finding solutions.

Option Seven

The answer might be as simple as using proximics to shut the complainer down — stand near or sit next to him or her, or change the setup during a break so you will now be seated next to that person after the break.

If someone else in the group has a lot more power over the complainer, use proximics by seating the complainer next to the person. Sometimes a complainer is more inclined to gripe sitting across from the boss than sitting next to the boss.

Option Eight

Get the group to police the situation. If the complainer is out of line and the group feels it, get the group to ask the person to keep focused on solutions. Try: "It might only be me, but does anyone feel we are doing too much stopping and focusing on side issues?"

If they concur, ask: "What should we do about it?"

Usually they come up with an appropriate way of dealing with the issue. Notice it's not singling the person out but dealing with the behavior.

If the complainer is the boss and the group is hesitant to respond, preface your questions with, "We agreed in our ground rules that we would focus on one topic or issue at a time, didn't we?" After confirmation, go into the questions as above.

Option Nine

Try a little humor. Make a light joke about the number of complaints, issues or problems raised.

Maybe make an obvious and focused glance at your watch and say, "You know, maybe we should change our ending time to one or two hours later if we are going to cover all these additional issues!" Then ask them to see if they want to go that long or limit the issues to those agreed upon up-front.

Other simple methods of weaving in humor, which could be embodied in the ground rules, include:

- Placing a squirt pistol on the table and if someone brings up another problem before the group solves the existing one, the first person to notice can give that person one squirt. (Obviously, this has to be part of the ground rules.)
- Each person contributing a solution gets a white poker chip and anyone bringing up a problem gets a red chip. The person with the most red chips has to clean up after the meeting and the person with the most white chips gets a prize of some sort. (This is assuming you are not in a problem-identifying facilitation.)
- Have everyone wad up a piece of paper and set a new ground rule that anyone who comes up with a negative or a complaint for the next hour gets beaned by all the people who catch it.

Option Ten

Be direct. I don't like this approach because it can turn a person off and maybe even some of the others, certainly those who are allied with the complainer. However, with repeat offenders, it can be an effective method.

"Jim, that isn't really the issue now, is it? Let's stay focused, okay? Thank you."

"Mary, we agreed not to bring up new issues until we solve the one we are currently discussing. Please hold your thought/comment until later. Are you okay with that? Thank you."

Or even, "That's a car park issue, isn't it? Let's set it aside until later or save it for another meeting."

These SFOs are not exhaustive, but they seem to work well for those of us Mining For Gold™. Once again, having thorough and specific ground rules up-front makes dealing with most of these issues a lot *easier* than trying to fix one or all of them later.

Methods of Facilitation

"There's more than one way to get things done.
Let's be creative!"

Most common facilitators only use one type of facilitation technique. Each facilitation is the same. Each time they will stand in front of the group, run through the ground rules, make a parking lot poster to store any issues to be covered later and then get started.

There are literally millions of possibilities to help us Mine For Gold™ if we only let our creativity come out to play in the design phase. This chapter contains several different methodologies of Mining For Gold™ to get you thinking and to spur some creative thoughts.

Divide and Conquer

We've used this method often where there are two groups in one, both with completely different agendas.

First, we break them up into subgroups. Their assignment in each group is to come up with a list of arguments to present to the other group or groups. This helps them crystallize their arguments before presenting them to the entire group.

When the information starts to flow, it's amazing how quickly people understand the points made. Then, in concert with the group presenting, all groups come up with either solutions or commitments to prevent the recurrence of the problems cited or certain behaviors on the part of the "adversarial" group.

Example 1: When facilitating a discussion of bosses and their personal assistants (PAs), we put all bosses in a corner and all PAs in the opposite corner.

Their assignment – to come up with a top ten list of the things their counterparts do that upset them. The comments are fast, furious and fun.

When we bring them together, we either have them share one point each as they go through the list or each group takes turns to share what they dislike about the other group.

It is amazing how some PAs who would never DARE tell their bosses something, will openly share with colleagues. When colleagues share as a group, this gives them the strength and confidence to share all they need to "get off their collective chests" and the bosses finally get to hear what they need to hear. Likewise, bosses who may have shared the same issues over and over and were never taken seriously now have their entire group agreeing on the issues which bother ALL of them. This process allows both parties to air their grievances within a safe environment while learning to see the point of view of the other party(s) helps all parties to resolve conflicts or issues.

Example 2: In our Creative Training workshops, in order to help trainers understand how their bad habits could cost them credibility and effectiveness, we address male trainers and female trainers separately while they are sitting in the same group.

The instructions are, "Guys, sit back and relax. Take out a chaw of tobacco. Put your feet up. It's the women's turn to share what male trainers do that irritate you women with their appearance, demeanor, content or stories." Then the females share. After the females vent their frustrations, we turn to the males and say, "Women, put your feet up. Take out a chaw of tobacco. It's the men's turn to share what female trainers do that irritate you guys with their appearance, demeanor, content or stories." Then the males share.

Caveat: We are not advocating chewing tobacco. It's just a figure of speech and it adds a bit of fun.

Amazingly, some of the same behaviors come up all the time and some are so outlandish, you wonder how anyone could ever do them in a training or teaching situation.

Comments flow easily as each group is not ALLOWED to speak while they are in the hot seat. If one group speaks out of turn in defense of their gender, a little humorous reminder will usually set you back on track.

If the group is a little quiet to start with, a quick example from the facilitator primes the pump and usually gets the ball rolling. You can use this to generate discussion on controversial topics, open communications, as an ice-breaker, team-building and bonding exercise or just as a change of pace if the energy is dropping. Obviously, this can be used as a training exercise in addition to facilitation.

In either Divide and Conquer exercise, each group makes specific commitments at the end to change certain behaviors and it usually ends up being one of the best-loved exercises in the facilitation.

Mix and Match

Mix and Match is another discussion-based exercise where you break into small groups. Strive to attain a balance of participants with different roles in the organization in each of the small groups - managers, engineers, sales, accounting, etc.

Give each group either the same task or different tasks to complete. If the groups are given different tasks, then their component parts can be married to a whole in a collective group exercise immediately after the small group session.

The advantage of this method of facilitation is the great diversity of ideas and perspectives. It also tends to foster teamwork and spark friendships and understanding. Mix and Match works best with noncontroversial topics.

Example 1: When you are having trouble getting input from a larger group, you can use Mix and Match to draw out ideas in subgroups.

Let's say you have a group that needs to come up with a new mission statement. Instead of trashing it out for hours in a group of say 18 leaders, divide them into smaller groups.

Set them up with a blend of people from each department, putting them in four groups with four or five people in each group. Make sure each group has a ripchart™ and pens.

Give each group the same assignment: To come up with a new mission statement in just 20 minutes to be recorded on the ripchart™ provided so that it's large enough for everyone to read. The tight timeframe forces everyone to think on their feet and usually produces great ideas quickly.

Bringing them back together as a whole group, have a representative from each group read each of the four versions or quickly photocopy each of the four versions during a coffee break and distribute them.

Then have them comment on which statement or parts of statements they prefer and why. Notice this keeps comments in the positive.

They are not allowed to comment on their own statement at first so they have to recognize the other groups' work. This is important or they may start "defending their turf", protecting what they have prepared.

In an hour or less, the new statement can be adopted. The exciting aspect of this method is that everyone can go away with the feeling that they have contributed to the creation of the statement or were part of the thought process in the final product.

Example 2: When you have a controversial issue to facilitate, say, budget cutting, everyone will tend to protect their own rice bowl. You can use Mix and Match to help you come up with more creative and realistic solutions.

First, as before, divide a cross functional group into smaller but balanced groups. Have each group come up with a top ten list of ways to cut costs. Smaller groups tend to compromise faster.

Give them a short time to come up with their list, maybe just 15 minutes. The pressure cooker gives us good results in a short time.

At the end of the time, if they don't have all ten, it doesn't matter. Work with what they DO have. The "Top Ten" list is just a small pressure cooker made popular by comedian David Letterman. In Asia, we might make it a "Top Eight" list for a Chinese group or some other number that is "fatt" (Cantonese for "luck") or auspicious for the country in which you are working.

Bring them back to the whole group and go through the lists, taking one idea at a time from each group to discuss the idea's feasibility. This is critical because if you deal with one list after another, eventually, the last group will feel left out because everyone has "stolen" most or all of their ideas.

As you gain input as to whether the ideas have possibilities or merit further discussion, make a separate list from the many. You conclude the exercise by coming up with assignments or topics for further discussion.

Friend and Foe

Friend and Foe is another way to get the discussion started. Take a group and divide them into two smaller groups at random or with a balance if you feel that is necessary.

One group is given the assignment to accept or defend an issue or position with every possible argument, good or bad. The other group is to reject the same issue or position with equal fervor. Each group is to list all the arguments on ripcharts™ accordingly.

When time is up, each group will present their "answers" or "reasons" one by one.

The Miner For Gold™ can either:

1. stop them at the end of each reason and have the entire group debate its validity or
2. wait until all ideas are presented on ONE side and then the whole group debates what they have just heard or
3. wait until both sides have presented and have the group now select the best arguments based upon their merits.

Because the participants are grouped at random or given their positions to defend at random, they have to make a case for that position, even if they actually believe the opposite. This forces them to think at a deeper level and will help them "hear" what their opponents have to say.

This exercise unnerves some people, but almost always helps them see the opponent's side of the argument.

The fact that some of the people have to shoot holes into what would normally be their own arguments likewise helps them understand what the opposition has been saying all along.

Skenectics

For the braver gold miner, you may wise to take brainstorming to the limit. Skenectics is just the tool to use for that purpose. Developed for advanced creative purposes, it is an adjunct to brainstorming and helps you expand play and creativity.

First, take a group of ideas you have already brainstormed. Then take them one-at-a-time and further expand them. Say, "Let's take these ideas and see how much further we can push them. Push them even to the sublime."

In Skenectics, you start to throw our "get fired" solutions. These ideas are SO off-the-wall that if anyone took you seriously, you'd "get fired".

This exercise takes ideas to the sublime. Skenectics would take an idea, say: "Let's form groups to come up with solutions for us" to its "get fired" limit: "Let's get our competitors to come up with the solutions for us to defeat them."

While many of the ideas developed seem useless, the exercise expands the realm of possibilities and frees up thinking.

After the thinking is freed up and these "get fired" solutions are listed on a ripchart™, the group will now look for ways to implement the ideas generated.

In the above example about having competitors provide the solutions, maybe a group will determine that looking at the competitor's magazine advertisements will provide the team with the answer(s) to the next marketing or engineering problem. Hence, the competitors DID tell them exactly how to defeat them.

I read a story once (sorry, can't quote the source), where NASA was brainstorming on how to solve the project handed them by President John F. Kennedy – to put a man on the moon in ten years. Standard brainstorming was coming up short on solutions for how to put a man on the moon and they applied Skenectics. One of the problems they were dealing with was how to make the correct calculations for rocket burns. Specifically, it would take 1,000 people with calculators 1,000 hours each to come up with the answer.

In a Skenectics session, someone threw up the idea, "We'll just make a machine to think up the answer for us!" Did someone say, "Computer?"

The wackiness of the exercise also keeps the group's energy up so in addition to great ideas, it makes the facilitator's job a lot easier.

Using Proximics, Kinesics and Eye Contact to Make the Mining For Gold™ Facilis (easy to do)!

It is not always the words we use that make our mining operations work or fail. The way the Miner For Gold™ stands, sits, looks, moves, gestures and pauses plays a pivotal role as well. All nonverbal aspects of communication come into play and need to be considered in every facilitation.

Over the years, we all have developed our own information filters. These filters evolve over time based upon age, race, gender, education as well as country-state-community-family culture. These filters open and close our minds and hearts in every communication in which we play a part. At times we are all open to suggestions and new ideas and at other times, we tend to close down and not listen.

As Mining For Gold™ is about people communicating, the miner's knowledge and control of these filters is vital to the success of the process. If you can open your participants' filters right from the beginning and keep them open, an amazing amount of communication can take place.

If you or someone in the group does something offensive, instills fear, anger, mistrust, jealousy, skepticism, envy, confusion or conflict in one or more of the participants, it can become a nightmare to get people to open up and really participate.

While truly being able to read people can take a lifetime, being able to communicate with others really has to do with keeping your information filters open and finding ways of opening up the filters of others.

How to stay focused on people's filters, helping you read them or having them understand you and also each other can be learned in a short while. Here are a few simple tools for opening up people's filters and these can instantly make you a better communicator and facilitator. This skill makes Mining For Gold™ a lot easier.

Smile

First, let's start with something quite basic, the smile. Having traveled the globe, it's struck me how one gesture in one culture can mean something totally different in another. For example, the "thumbs up" sign means something positive in most western cultures. In some cultures, it may mean something rude.

While most people believe a nod indicates agreement or "yes", in some African cultures, this means "no".

A smile, however, means the same thing in every culture on the planet. It means warmth, acceptance, appreciation, that you are happy, you like the person you are smiling at - all of which are positive.

If you smile at the participants in your facilitation, you are sending a lot of positive messages. It is a conditioned response for you to like someone smiling at you. It means good things. As a result, a smile will open people's filters and get them to hear and share more freely.

For those of you who have not studied psychology, a conditioned response is an automatic response we give when confronted by a stimulus. It's like if someone eats a sour lemon in front of you, you start to pucker up and your mouth begins to produce more saliva as you think about how sour that lemon is and how it tastes as that lemon juice dribbles down the person's chin. (By the way, do you have any extra saliva in your mouth now?) *That* is a conditioned response.

CAUTION: Some facilitators will totally disagree with us on this point. They encourage facilitators to NEVER smile. They believe you show bias when you smile as you will tend to smile more at people you like or who share information you agree with and not at those you dislike or with whom you disagree.

We suggest you strive to be consistent. Again, we found it a lot easier (and healthier) to smile a lot even at people we don't particularly like than it is NOT to smile at people we DO like.

Proximics

As discussed in a previous chapter, Proximics is how close we are in proximity to the people around us. Proximics can open people up or shut them down.

To understand the role of proximics, consider your culture or the culture of the people you are in the process of "mining".

In Singapore, Malaysia and much of Asia, most people are comfortable with one to one-and-a-half arm's length between themselves and the person they are talking to. This is similar in New Zealand, Australia and North America.

Anything closer is an uncomfortable distance. If you are too far away, they may feel you are "distant". This is a good distance rule to respect people's "personal space".

Exception: If you are dealing with the opposite sex, you might want to back away an additional half arm's length to a full arm's length.

Backing away opens their communication filters and allows them to share their golden ideas.

In Japan, add half an arm's length to two arm's lengths depending upon the authority the person holds in the organization. The more power they have, the further away you should stand. For friends, you can stand closer.

In India, most of the Arab world and much of the Mediterranean, an arm's length or even closer is comfortable, except, again, between men and women.

In any given culture, if the group is small, you'll probably want to sit in a strategic spot, near the source with the most power and maybe near anyone who might cause some trouble.

Standing or sitting next to a person of power gives you greater standing within the group. Have you ever heard the expression, "He's my right hand man/woman"? Many people's filters "open to power".

While you may not need this power, just having it may help you handle someone who wants to dominate or cause disruptions.

A quick glance at the person in power may encourage him or her to say something to bring the group back into control and close some filters that are too open.

If the person in power is the problem and starts to dominate the discussion, you only need to lean closer to him or her which tends to quiet them down.

You are also in a position to deflect the group's attention away from that person as all eyes will be on the power person speaking next to you. If you make a comment, the eyes will turn to you and then, by simply standing or moving away as you talk, you would have shifted the attention away from the dominator.

If you are not sure where to stand at the start of a facilitation, take a tip from John T. Malloy. In his book *Live For Success*, Malloy noted that people of power tend to step into a room and move immediately to the left. Malloy theorizes they do this so they can see who comes and goes, exit if they believe it's not worth their while and be able to "hang out" with people of similar power. This is a good proximics position for a Gold Miner to take.

If the meeting consists of a larger group, you might want to take a "stage" position in front of the room, with a chair handy so as to be able to sit down and become part of the group. Bear in mind that if you take a stage position, being too far from the group makes you seem distant while getting too close can be overbearing.

CAUTION: Whatever distance may seem appropriate in your culture for protecting personal space when both people are standing may not apply if you are standing and the person near to you is seated. That appropriate distance usually doubles. Most common facilitators forget this and stand too close to someone while asking him or her a question. After getting no response from the person, they think, "Why didn't he or she share anything?" Remember, to open their filters, they must *feel* comfortable.

Open Them Up and Shut Them Down

Knowing that proximics can impact people's comfort level and hence their ability to open up their communication filters is a powerful bit of information that bears repeating.

Let's say you have someone who's talking too much or acting inappropriately in a meeting. Just moving close to them and standing next to them when someone else is speaking will very often get them to close their filters, without you saying a single word. Likewise, most miners make the mistake of being too close to someone when they want them to share.

Please keep in mind that the #1 fear for most people is public speaking. Calling on someone by name, looking at them, standing close to them will not only make them feel uncomfortable and want to shut down, it will *also* direct every set of eyes in the room in the direction of that person.

With a room full of people staring at you, few have the confidence to share as openly as they would like, myself included.

"What? Mike, you are a professional speaker, trainer, facilitator and inventor of Mining For Gold™. You get nervous when people stare at you?"

Sure! I don't mind it from a platform delivering a well-planned talk or presentation. I don't mind it when conducting a gold mining operation as I've prepared and know the process. Responding to a question I was not given time to prepare a statement about is disconcerting.

The reason it's troubling is because of the unknown. I don't always know *how* that person wants me to respond. I don't know if I understood the question correctly. I might not have been paying perfect attention and may have felt a bit embarrassed that thoughts of my family or some work situation came into my conscious mind. I don't know if I'll say something that could offend someone. I don't know if I'll be as coherent as I'm *expected* to be as a "professional".

Because people have the fear of the unknown and the fear of making mistakes, they often will not open up in a situation where those fears can become a reality. When it is one-to-one or in small groups, most are not as self-conscious. But in larger groups, anxiety sets in.

This is how a Miner For Gold™ can get someone to open up by walking to the opposite end of the room, making momentary eye contact with the person you want to talk to and then asking them a series of questions; starting with an easy one, building up in greater difficulty. In this way, you gradually draw the person out and help them feel comfortable.

When the person is more comfortable speaking and finally starts responding to the *real* question you want to ask, simply glancing away at another participant takes the focus off that person even more. Most of the eyes will be on YOU and NOT on the participant, making it easier for him or her to continue speaking.

This added space you give to people relaxes them and allows them to open their filters. Believe me, proximics is a POWERFUL tool.

Kinesics

Kinesics does it all. Kinesics is the technical term for body language. Body language can either make people nervous, shutting them down, or it can relax them, opening their filters.

Nervous people, as we have stated, do not open up. So it is essential for a Miner of Gold™ to determine if your own body language is making people nervous and uncomfortable or relaxed and open.

Stance and Posture

Let's take, for example, the two most comfortable positions for a typical male: arms folded or hands in their pockets. In seminars worldwide, I'll fold my arms and ask the audience what message this sends. Attendees respond with words or phrases like cold, arrogant, aloof, closed, uninterested, superior, not open, over confident and the like.

All of which are incredibly negative responses to a very common stance or posture.

Although you may fold your arms for very innocent reasons – you are cold, nervous, self-conscious (the real message could in fact be a physical reaction to the environment) – yet all these unintended messages are coming across as well.

The "hands-in-pockets" posture is a bit different, with responses ranging from relaxed to lazy, unprofessional to profane (don't ask!).

The bottom line is – either posture could cost you as the gold miner by setting up your group to NOT respond to your questions even though you are truly sincere, interested, honest and humble.

Contrast the two previous postures with a simple, erect posture stance with arms outstretched at a low 35° angle, palms facing forward, towards the group. What does that posture say?

Typical audience responses are "open, friendly, welcoming, inviting, down-to-earth and listening". NEVER is there a negative comment or response to this stance and gesture.

Equally important, your posture and gestures while seated can make a huge difference. Should you lean forward or sit back?

Interestingly, what works in sales works well in facilitation. If you want someone to open up, leaning forward shows interest. Learning back tends to make you look "passive" or uninvolved.

The problem is that they tend to look at you so you become the focus instead of the other participants. So to open someone up, start by leaning forward towards him or her and then as he or she starts sharing, lean back and look at the other participants. (I'll explain this below when we cover the subject of eye contact.)

Pointing Versus Acknowledging

To point or not to point; that is the question. Actually, it's HOW to point. In Asia, people point with their thumbs. In North America, people tend to point with their index fingers. When it comes to Mining For Gold™, NEITHER is good.

To recognize people, try looking at their eyes intently to let them know that you are looking at them. Next, call them by name and gesture with the back of your hand motioning towards them as you acknowledge them. A "rowing motion" with the hand works well for this, raising the hand to chest level, extending it to the person you wish to acknowledge and dropping it back to your waist as you pull the arm back to your body. It's a gesture that says, "Please share."

Once they start speaking, feel free to gesture to the rest of the group to ensure participants look and speak to each other and not to you. After all, THEY should be the focus.

You can gesture to the whole group by using a palm up, flat hand small circular motion towards the main body of the group. "What is the group's thinking on that?" would be an appropriate choice of words to accompany this gesture.

Alternatively, you might gently touch someone's shoulder in the main body of participants while looking at the others in the group. Don't expect that person to talk while you are standing there touching his or her shoulder. It is just a "wake up" gesture. Now call their names, walk away as you ask them an easy question. As the person responds, look at him or her briefly and ask the real question you wanted to ask, glancing away at others in the group. You'll find that more people will be comfortable sharing this way and the golden nuggets will begin to flow.

Using the right body posture and gestures either opens your participants up or shuts them down. It is not to be taken lightly.

I'd suggest you practice open gestures in front of a mirror on a regular basis and video yourself in every facilitation. (Do this discretely. Many people "clam up" when a camera is in the room.) Play back the video on fast-forward to see if your gestures and posture were inviting or limiting discussion. Fast-forward dramatizes the movements and makes gestures easier to spot.

Eye Contact

The eyes have it. During my life and in my various careers as an association president, business owner, speaker, trainer, salesman and account executive, I've learned the importance of eye contact in the Western, Asian, European, South American and African context.

In much of Asia and the West, a lack of eye contact gives the impression we are stupid, shifty, deceitful, dishonest, shy, unintelligent, disinterested, unsure, slow-witted, dull, lying or worse.

Direct eye contact in most of Asia is seen as honest, intelligent, caring, interested, self assured, positive, caring, attentive and full of even more positive inferences.

Hence, looking at your attendees allows you to gain their trust and they will be more inclined to open up to you. The problem is, when Mining For Gold™, you don't want them to look at you; you want them to look at each other.

Seeing is believing. If you look at a person while they speak, they will continue to look at you. If you are giving a speech, it makes sense to focus on individuals one at a time to create a tight bond or connection. This *must be* the starting point in Mining For Gold™.

First, make eye contact out of respect, to get them to relax, believe it is safe to share and feel comfortable in sharing. It helps them feel that they have a one-to-one connection with you and are just speaking to one person. This relaxes them and opens their filters.

Second, as they begin to open up, glance away to others in the group so they will likewise look at each other instead of you. After all, you are trying to get them to share with each other, not conduct a dialog with you.

In many other cultures, eye contact has a different meaning. To the Japanese, for example, eye contact is seen as confrontational or disrespectful. You can still make eye contact for a split moment to establish contact after which you should glance away to respect that person and his or her culture. Looking towards the group but not at any one individual for more than a second or two can culturally accommodate these people into the Mining For Gold™ model.

Ergonomics

Ergonomics relates to the physical and environmental factors that influence our behavior. If you want people to open up and be intimate, we need to create an environment where they are comfortable and relaxed.

To accomplish this, participants need to be fairly close to one another, but not too close. Spacing between seats is critical. Knowing your group, determine how much personal space they need and set up the room accordingly - if there is too much space between them, participants may become non-participants; too little space and they can be uncomfortable or even irritable.

First, consider your group size when you choose the room. Don't take the first available room or automatically go for the main conference room. Packing them into a small room may be an efficient use of space, but this may cause them to clam up.

Putting them in one little corner of a huge room may afford them tons of elbow room but the space itself becomes a sponge, sucking up the energy and the interaction potential. Look until you find a space that is "just right" for the purpose of your facilitation.

Tables can put distance between people and make them feel cold or disconnected. Some people feel uncomfortable without one as they have trouble facing people. This is where you have to know the group you are going to facilitate ahead of time.

Pick the size of the table or the lack thereof for your facilitation to accomplish what you set out to do given the size of your group, level of confidence of the people attending, the topic to be discussed and the need to write or hold materials.

Lighting impacts results as well. A dark room makes it hard for people to open up while a bright room tends to keep them awake and sharing, opening their filters. Many hotel meeting rooms are way too dark; designed for intimate banquets. Inspect rooms well in advance to ensure that you have a bright, appropriately sized room for your group.

If you want creativity, don't put them in a "bored room". Put them in a room that encourages creativity like the cafeteria, coffee shop or maybe outside sitting under a tree for a little enlightenment.

A room that's too cold will cause them to close up and shiver but a warm room is worse, putting them to sleep.

Suggestion: Set the room temperature just one degree cooler than would normally be comfortable. Better to err on the cool side than the warm, sleepy side. Plus, the more bodies you fit into a room, the more heat they generate, raising room temperatures dramatically.

Ergonomics can make or break a facilitation. Using smiles, proximics, kinesics and ergonomics will really help you in opening your participants' filters, making your job of Mining For Gold™ a lot easier.

Podolinsky's Five Power Points of Positive Participation

"You shouldn't have to drag it out of them!"

I t is facilis ("easy to do") to get people to open up and share if we do the right things right. It is also difficult or next to impossible if we do the wrong things or the right things at the wrong time as facilitators.

Mining For Gold™ makes it easy for us to do the right things if we apply these basic tools at the right time.

Here are Podolinsky's Five Power Points of Positive Participation developed over 20 odd years to help you with your next facilitation.

Participation Point #1

Take a tip from Outward Bound™ and "Challenge by Choice". Everyone signing up is expected to participate, but no one is forced to do anything. Once a challenge is laid down, they are highly encouraged to take part in the activity.

Peer "pressure" or "encouragement" along with the course leader's encouragement gets MOST people to fully participate in the activity. Likewise, if you challenge the participants to decide if they choose to get involved or participate, you can get some amazing results.

Here are some suggestions of approaches you may want to consider to get the group involved by challenging them to choose to participate.

1. "Now you don't have to share… and if you don't, it won't be held against you. It WILL take longer to get the solution and you may not be happy with the solution the group decides upon. As a result, if you want to be happy with the result, it would be great to have your full participation. As such, is it fair for me to ask people to participate who may not have had a chance to contribute yet? How many of you agree with this?" Anyone not raising their hands should be asked "Why?"; 99.9 percent of the time, all hands are raised.

2. "If you don't agree or disagree with something said, silence is often taken as acceptance. Having said that, for our exercise today, if you remain silent, we'll be able to safely assume you agree. So if you DON'T offer an idea or suggestion, agreement or disagreement, we'll just sign your name to whatever the rest of us who are participating decide and it will be presented as having your FULL backing. If this is NOT agreeable to you, simply share your input at the appropriate time and we'll take all your ideas and comments into account."

   Some may find this too harsh or too edgy. Fine. Don't use it.

   But we've found that it pushes people's buttons and gets them to open up a lot more. When they DO share, we reward their participation and in return, there's even more sharing. By the end of the exercise, they will have forgotten that the meeting had started off on such a "raw" note.

3. A simple way of gaining input is to simply go around the table(s) after each major debate for each person to comment on what has been discussed.

Rules like, "You can't use anyone else's exact words" can make it more of an individual commitment as they have to put it in their own words. This practice sometimes adds fun but certainly takes more time than just having people "rubber stamp" the ideas someone else had already shared.

4. "The other group..." is an outright challenge. If you are hoping to conjure ideas from more than one group, stating the success of the other group and how fast they did it lays down the gauntlet for the group you are working with to do it BETTER. Some facilitators would NEVER use such a tactic as they believe time is needed for good results to occur.

We disagree and go back to our pressure cooker mentality. You get more done under pressure with better results.

A few also object to the use of a competitive environment as it does not foster team building. But hey, people love competitions. Ever heard of TEAM sports like football, rugby, cricket or netball?

Participation Point #2

Gain participation by demanding it outright! Just asking an individual to share is fine but it is best when asked "in fun".

"Doesn't that just disagree with what you said about 'Challenge by Choice?'"

Yes and no. When demanding for input, you ask for a volunteer to offer comments but make it very obvious as to whom you are asking. You either look at them, infer them by name, department or title. The key is, all this is done "IN FUN".

Sometimes we start off with, "We need an answer from someone who's highly intelligent, a true leader, a manager's manager, a fine human being in his or her own right..."

At this point they are usually laughing. Then ask someone by looking directly at him or her. That person usually responds with a smile, laugh, blush or sarcastic "yea right..." and shares his or her opinion. It works 80–90 percent of the time. If you still do not get an answer, try another method.

Asking a subgroup for input is a good tool to try. This puts pressure on that subgroup to share an idea. For example, ask, "Who is in-charge of...." When you get a response from that person(s), ask them for the information you need. If you think about it, they are already talking when they respond to your first non-threatening question so it's usually very easy to keep them talking till they answer your more pertinent questions.

Like many of our other techniques, some facilitators would disagree and say that the technique is too contrived or too facilitator-focused. But it works. Ultimately, the choice is up to you.

CAUTION: Refrain from calling on people by name. Once you call on someone by name, everyone settles into the mode of, "Oh, they are calling names for response. I'll wait until my name is called before I share". We found that this *kills* participation.

Participation Point #3

Gain participation by NEVER "stepping on" the participation you DO get. It bears repeating that no facilitator should ever say: "Wrong", "Bad idea", "That's not what we were looking for", "Maybe…" , "Are there any other better ideas?", etc. Any of these statements only serve to shut down the participant.

Instead, *feed* participation! Feed what they say with praise, reward, recognition, thanks, appreciation, non-lingual sounds of encouragement ("ahh", "ohh", "mmmm", "oh yea", "ah ha", "mmhmmm", "whoha!", "ya!", etc.) and enthusiasm or any other trick you can muster.

Some facilitators will disagree and insist you NEVER agree or reward participation because it is not the facilitator's job to agree or disagree as we are neutral parties in the process.

The nay sayers are partially right but mostly wrong. We are supposed to be neutral, but in reality, there is no such thing.

A newspaper is supposed to be neutral, but read three newspapers covering the same story and you'll get three different views on the same story.

A scientist, in carrying out his experiments, is supposed to assume the null hypothesis, but in reality, he makes the assumption while attempting to PROVE it's NOT true.

You as a Miner of Gold™ WILL be biased. Any attempt to think you are neutral is your first big mistake. Instead, acknowledge that you WILL be biased and then work to minimize your influence. Strive to praise and acknowledge all participation *equally*.

Participation Point #4

Rewards. In the case of rewards, reward the participation, not the content. Get excited about their sharing, not necessarily about the quality of the input. Get equally excited if they say "yes" or "no", "up" or "down", "buy" or "sell". In short, reward the progress and participation, NOT the content.

As psychology has taught us, what is rewarded will be repeated; what is ignored or punished will disappear. Make sure you reward the participation or you can be assured that you will see less and less of it. Rewarding ALL participation will almost guarantee more participation from everyone in the future.

Will you make mistakes and show partiality? Of course! You are human. Just be professional to minimize it.

Now the next question is: What kinds of rewards can we offer? Many people think that money and gifts are the only rewards of value. Actually, there are many rewards we can offer, in particular, verbal, physical and results rewards.

Verbal Rewards

Verbal Rewards are easier to distribute. Verbal rewards include:

1. "Thanks for sharing that…"
2. "Good input"
3. "Nice idea"
4. "Well said"
5. "Appreciate the sharing"
6. "Yes, and…"
7. "Wow… this is good. More please."
8. "We see why you say that. More please."
9. "Ah. And…"
10. "Great. And…"
11. "Mmmm… And…"
12. "All right. Some more please."
13. "Can you all agree? Thanks. What else?"
14. "Would the rest see it that way (to an obviously right answer)? Thank you so much."
15. "Yea… we hear you."
16. "Super. Next."

17. To an obviously unpopular sharing, say something like, "Hey, thanks for sharing that. It obviously took some courage to share an idea not everyone agrees with. We need more dissenting views to keep the discussion germane and alive. Thanks so much for sharing." and so forth.

Don't use the same words all the time as it sounds boring. Boring will get you bored participants. Be fun, alive and fresh and this will get you more lively feedback. Remember, variety is the spice of life.

Physical Rewards

Physical Rewards can be in the form of sweets and give-aways. We usually toss out Tootsie Rolls®, Tootsie Roll Pops®, Dots®, Smarties®, Laffy Taffy®, etc. We also pass out stretchy stress men, stress balls, stress rocks, incentives with a theme (stress balls in stress programs), smiley faces, smiley key chains, smiley pencils, sticky hands and feet (used for taking papers off other people's desks), bubble makers, etc. Some folks would think these "toys" are inappropriate.

Surprisingly, given a choice, half of our adult participants say "anything", the other half requests sweets or a specific toy. Very few tell us they want nothing at all.

In facilitating groups comprising top executives, they rarely EAT any of the sweets. Instead, they keep the pile in front of them to show they are "winning" the game.

Executive secretaries or entry-level managers usually consume the sweets as soon as they get them but they sometimes prefer to put the warm fuzzy "critters" on their computer or telephone back at their desk, office or cubicle.

Some just tolerate the give-aways until they go home and give them to their children.

One returning participant admitted he thought it was foolishness until he gave the gifts to his son who immediately jumped up into his lap and gave him a big hug and a kiss saying, "Papa, you must be really smart. Thank you SO much."

He said to me, "So today I will answer TWICE as many questions and give TWICE as much feedback."

This tells us that rewards work and frankly, as long as you get the results you want, why not try it? We have been using this technique since 1982 and have had fewer than six complaints and *thousands* of compliments.

Results

Results can also be a form of reward.

Some suggestions would include:

1. Post on a wall the progress of the group to show what they've accomplished so far.
2. Place in your organization's newsletter the group's photo and a write-up about the progress made IMMEDIATELY after the facilitation to reward their participation. (The NEXT facilitation will be even more active.)
3. Ask the BIG BOSS to step in during the program to thank them for a job well done, sharing the key thoughts developed thus far.

In short, when preparing rewards, think beyond the facilitation room and think of the entire effect of a facilitation on the participant's work, family, career or job. Finally, take the program out of your hands and think of rewards from their perspective.

1. How about finishing early if there is a lot of input or their main goal is accomplished?
2. How about buying them lunch if they finish prior to lunchtime?
3. How about arranging a special dinner or drinks after the meeting?
4. How about agreeing to let them come in late or leave early on any particular workday of their choice for TOTAL participation by the ENTIRE group?

Here again, we are limited only by our own creativity.

Should we have to reward employees for doing their job? Of course not… as long as we live in a perfect world.

Since we don't live in anything near perfection, why fight human psychology? If it works, doesn't cost much or anything at all, wouldn't we be foolish NOT to use *every* tool in our Mining For Gold™ tool chest?

Participation Point #5

NOISE! That's right, noise. As alluded to earlier, we call it facilitation room inertia. Similar to the law of inertia, a room that's quiet will tend to stay quiet. A room that's noisy will tend to stay noisy. If you want a group to open up, get a little noise going in the room.

"Noise" comes from people laughing at silly props displayed, music playing softly in the background during discussions or loudly as they enter the room to build enthusiasm, a bit of humor from a joke or funny anecdote, you closing your eyes and pretending to snore for a brief moment if they don't answer a question (the laughter creates the real noise), etc.

Noise also comes from breaking the group into smaller groups, stretch breaks, short games and exercises such as you playing "devil's advocate" and presenting an off-the-wall position or just brainstorming while standing to change the energy.

Most people have some thoughts they'd like to share but don't know if people will laugh, listen, boo, accept or reject their ideas. In reality people could actually end up applauding them and their ideas, but this fact rarely enters the realm of consciousness for most people. As such, they will not break the deafening silence that follows, "What are your thoughts?" or "Any other ideas?".

Remember, if you create a little noise, the participants will start to speak because you've made it comfortable for them by breaking the silence. When they are comfortable, Gold Mining becomes facilis.

Paraphrasing, Feedback, Summarizing and Questioning Techniques

"In other words ... "

W hen Mining For Gold™, one of the essential skills is to rephrase what they are saying, have said or are trying to say. It means you as a facilitator will have to listen to the thought, content, emotion, hidden agendas and underlying points being made.

While this really takes a ton of practice (for which there is no substitute), here's a primer to help you out and get you started.

"But" and "However"

First off, don't use the words "but..." or "however...".

When we use either of these words, we can turn someone off or embarrass him or her, shutting down future communications not only from that individual and possibly the entire group. You would also have just erased what came before the "but" or "however", which is usually something you want them to retain.

For example, "That was a good idea, *but* I'm sure there is another approach." What they hear is, "That was worthless... who's got something significant to say?"

Likewise, "You are a great participant, *however*, your constant input is making it difficult to draw other people out." ALL that is heard is, "YOU are making it difficult."

Instead use, "That is much appreciated. Thank you! *And* some additional ideas?", this builds the person up and acknowledges his or her contribution. What they hear from us is "Good idea. Let's get more good ideas like this last one."

For example, "You have some great ideas *and* I'm sure everyone else has same great ideas for us as well."

An exception is when you do NOT want them to remember what you have said before the "but".

Example: If someone has not contributed all morning and now starts sharing, you might say, "Wow... that's great. You know, you have not shared much in the morning but now you are coming up with these great ideas. Thank you!" The "but" erases the negative image in their mind and supports and maybe even rewards the positive behavior now.

Paraphrase

When Mining For Gold™, you could also use paraphrases that will help the person communicate their thoughts better without making them look foolish. These phrases will also assist the participants in understanding what was said without making either the person sharing or the person(s) hearing feel foolish, dim-witted or out of synch.

Some examples of good paraphrasing openers include:

1. "What I hear you saying is..."
2. "If I understand you correctly..."
3. "In other words..."
4. "Like you are/were saying..."
5. "That's a bit like..."
6. "Yes, and..."

All of these phrases have their own merits. Not repeating the same phrase or phrases will make the facilitation more interesting. Participants will not hear a "formulaic" approach as a result. Instead, we become "invisible" to the process rather than becoming the "focus" of it.

CAUTION: Avoid saying "what you said was...". Putting words in someone's mouth is off-putting, often rude and we could be incorrect, Instead, try "If I heard you correctly..." or "Correct me if my interpretation is incorrect, what I heard you say was...".

Summarize and Restate

For proactive summarization and restatement skills, rarely, if ever, say, "In summary..." or "In conclusion..." As soon as these phrases leave your mouth, most folks tune out and stop listening. They figure, "I've heard this before so why bother listening." And they trip off to some romantic fantasy, some irrelevant trivia or to their next pressing work duty.

Rather than telling participants that you are now going to repeat what they have already heard, here are some ways to summarize without saying "In summary" or some derivation of it.

1. "What we've accomplished/done/said so far is..."
2. "Pulling this all together..."
3. "As we've stated..."
4. "What we've come up with..."
5. "Your approach so far has been..."
6. "Looking at our results thus far..."
7. "Examining our progress..."
8. "Tell me if I've got this right..."

Summarizing Exercises

Aside from these phrases, exercises form great summaries. The best ones focus not on what they have discussed, but what they will DO as a result of the time and energy invested in the facilitation.

Some summarization exercises include:

1. Go round the room and ask each person to share a commitment they are willing to make, one thought derived from the previous discussion, one key point the team agreed on, one specific action step the team came up with to achieve what the group has decided to do.

2. Go back to the ripchart™ pages on which the progress has been recorded and ask the group to prioritize the points or progress. This gets them focusing not only on what was discussed, but on the next step or steps they will need to take.

3. Similarly, if you are placing just one key thought per flip chart page, place them on a wall in order of progress to summarize without having to say it. Every time they see the wall, they are reviewing the steps of the process.

   Also, every time someone suggests they change the order of the pages, you are reviewing the entire process.

4. Go down each point and say, "To make sure we are in full agreement, share again please the action steps we'll all take as a result of our facilitation today. Make sure I didn't miss anything in recording your thoughts. This is also a good time to add anything that you feel or think might be missing."

This is essentially summarizing but it gives them another reason to participate to either share more or to prevent you "messing up" their efforts. Sneaky, but it works.

CAUTION: A few people do START listening when someone says, "In conclusion..." so it can become a paradoxical problem for us as "miners".

The reason some people start listening when they hear something like, "In summary..." is because they have tuned out the entire time before that. They have been trained at school and at meetings to ignore everything being said as there was no need to participate. All they had to do was just listen intently at the summary and internalize in a few moments what others struggled for hours or days to develop or learn.

If the latter is the case, we've not done our job as good facilitators. This shouldn't happen if we regularly engage everyone and not let anyone get away with "sleeping on the job".

Proactive Questioning

Asking PROACTIVE questions is also essential to deriving ongoing information from each participant.

Most facilitators will tell you to NEVER ask a closed-ended question. A closed-ended question can be answered with a "yes" or a "no".

Example: "Do you have an opinion on this topic?" Answer: "Yes."

Closed-ended questions can also be answered easily with a name, a date, a color or some other one- or two-word answer.

Example: "Who do you think the next team leader should be?" Answer: "Jane Tay."

Closed-ended questions give you little information and do not by themselves promote discussion or openness. That's why facilitators, professional trainers, sales gurus and professional speakers teach that we should *never* use such questions. Again, we disagree.

For most people, opening up and sharing is difficult. Answering a long or difficult question in front of colleagues, peers and the boss can be unnerving.

Many people think, "What if I make a mistake and look foolish?", "What if I offend someone?" or "What if the group disagrees with me?".

All these thoughts and more pass through their minds in a microsecond. As such, asking open-ended questions that require even a little thought can be VERY intimidating to some people.

Mining Questioning Technique

Use our Mining Questioning Technique (MQT) instead. Start with an easy "yes" or "no" type of closed-ended question. This gets them used to speaking and relaxes them. Follow up with one, two or several semi-closed-ended questions that they can answer with similar ease. This further relaxes them and allows you to gauge their level of comfort in sharing.

Now that they are comfortable with speaking in front of the group, you can ask them the pertinent questions, like a more difficult open-ended question. Using this approach, you will acquire a much higher percentage of open participation. You will also find a more relaxed, eloquent participant sharing with you and your team.

If you are asking an easy question with no pressure to answer, you may not need this multiple step approach. You can ask the question directly. But if the question is difficult, use the MQT approach.

To illustrate the point, imagine what would happen if you ask a person, "Please tell us in detail how management has been unfair in the past few months in determining how people get paid and who gets a raise (increment) or not."

MOST people would either refuse to answer or give an answer they think might make them look good to management as opposed to sharing the truth.

As an alternative approach, consider using the MQT approach. A MQT scenario might go something like this:

QUESTION: "I'm sorry, your name again?"

ANSWER: "Fred."

QUESTION: "Right, Fred. Thanks. Now Fred, do you find that management usually makes fair decisions about how much to pay each person and when they can get a raise in salary?"

ANSWER: "Well, not exactly."

QUESTION: "Thanks for your honesty. Would you say they make fair decisions always, sometimes or rarely?"

ANSWER: "Sometimes."

(The answer doesn't matter here as either way, you can proceed.)

QUESTION: "Thank you again for your honesty. Was it in the distant past or in the last few months that you have felt that they have been at times unfair in this practice?"

ANSWER: "Mostly in the past few months."

QUESTION: "Great, Fred. Really appreciate and admire you for sharing. Please share with us how it seems to have been unfair in the past few months."

At this point, 95 percent of the time the gates open up and the solid gold ideas flow. A single, open-ended question would have either shut the person up or probably rendered a response that would have been guarded or protective of the person's position.

"Think" and "Feel" Questions

To further the Mining For Gold™ process, ask both "thinking" and "feeling" kinds of questions. The thinking questions come from the logic centers of the brain.

Thinking questions include:

1. "What do you *think* about the merger?"
2. "What are your *thoughts* on that subject?"
3. "Which would be the *better choice*?"
4. "What would be the next *logical step*?"
5. "What is your *opinion* about…?"
6. "How would you *view*…?"
7. "Can you *envision*…?"
8. "What are your *conclusions* regarding…?"
9. "What would be the *results* of…?"
10. "What are your *ideas* regarding…?"
11. "If it were your *decision*, what would you do?"
12. "Have you *considered*…?"
13. "How would you *regard* the…?"
14. "Can you *imagine* a…?"
15. "What would you *conclude* from…?"
16. "Can you *remember* a…?"
17. "Would you *concur* with…?"
18. "Can you picture…?"

Feeling questions, on the other hand, come from the kinesthetic or emotional part of the brain sometimes referred to as "the heart". Feeling questions include:

1. "How do you *feel* about the merger?"
2. "What is your *reaction* to the cut back?"
3. "What is your *emotional reaction* to the change?"
4. "How will this action *affect*…?"
5. "What will be the *impact* of…?"
6. "Will you be *satisfied* if…?"
7. "Will you be *comfortable* with…?"
8. "Will you and the team be *happy* if we…?"
9. "What does that make you *want* to do?"
10. "Did this effort *touch* you in any way?"
11. "Are you *impressed* with…?"
12. "Do you *like* what is being done…?"
13. "What is your *sense* of …?"
14. "Are you able to *grasp* the…?"
15. "Do you *believe* this will…?"
16. "Can you get a *sense* of…?"
17. "Do you *perceive* this will…?"
18. "Are you able to *connect* with…?"

BOTH "What do you think?" and "How do you feel?" are great questions. Depending upon which one you use, you'll find yourself getting totally different answers.

For example, let's say you ask the following question: "What are your *thoughts* about the merger of the two banks?"

A worker might respond with something like: "Well, I *think* it's a great idea. It means better allocation of resources. It will give us more outlets in the marketplace. It will give us a competitive strength we didn't previously have and a more solid financial base."

Now ask that same person, "How do you feel about the merger?" You might hear this answer instead.

"I'm *scared* as hell that I might be fired. The larger bank taking over us has more than enough people in my position already."

Both were honest answers. Both were good answers. Both, however, came from a completely different part of the brain. If you really want to Mine for true Gold, not fools' gold, make sure you ask questions from the heart (FEELING) as well as the brain (THINKING).

CAUTION #1: If you ask, "What do you think...?" or "How do you feel...?", many times you'll get the exact same answer. If someone is in an emotional state, they will interpret what you are saying emotionally and translate "think" into "feel" and answer accordingly. If someone is in a very logical state, they may translate "feel" into "think". As such, using the variety of phrases we have already suggested AND pausing at the appropriate places (like after your "think" or "feel" word) in your questioning allow the addressee to hear what you are truly asking and he or she will respond, at your choosing, with either "thinking" or "feeling" answers.

CAUTION #2: Men and women are not identical in their word usage or perception of words. You may find that men tend to ask more "What do you think?" questions and women "How do you feel?" questions.

As BOTH are great questions we suggest that if you are male, make sure you ask an equal number of "feel" questions. If you are female, ask an equal number of "think" questions. As always, practicing both questioning techniques will make the questions flow more easily when you need them.

"What if" Questions

Asking "What if" questions is another great way to get people to open up and think out of their box.

Many times you'll find some participants resisting change, giving excuses or throwing up roadblocks to new possibilities. Obviously, if this negative thinking had been addressed in the ground rules, it might not be a problem later in the discussion.

Sometimes, even with the ground rules, some obstacles creep in to obstruct progress. "What if" questions are a great tool for getting around some of the toughest of barriers.

When someone throws a boulder in the road of progress, simply say something like:

1. "What if that barrier didn't exist, how would we proceed?"
2. "What if we DID have the budget, what would we do next?"
3. "What if the boss approves the plan, when would we start?"
4. "What if there were enough time, what would be the sequence of action steps to follow?"

Asking "What if...?" is a form of *possibility* thinking when Mining For Gold™. It also works very well for regular meetings for the prevention of problems before they occur.

Example: "What if one of our best customers asks for their money back after the warranty period is over, how would you handle it?"

After answering enough "What if" questions, most people will automatically handle new situations in a more professional manner as they've already mentally "practiced" the appropriate responses.

The MQT makes the questioning process flow and your mining operations more effective.

chapter

10

Dealing with Difficult
Participants

"# ? ! * # ! ! ?"

No matter how much you do up front to deal with difficult participants, you'll still end up having some who will not follow the
ground rules.

For some, it could be genetic; they were born contrarians. For others,
it may be a disorder of the brain or nervous system due to injury or
chemical poisoning during gestation or in early childhood.

Most, however, learned their negative group behaviors. Not only
were they learned, they were also reinforced. They learned that bullying
and just downright rude behavior often gets you exactly what you want.

Please keep in mind that when dealing with difficult participants (typically 1 percent of the population), the usual rules may not apply. With difficult people, a sterner, more direct approach may be necessary. This is why societies have police and countries have armies.

Here are some helpful hints to suppress, control or to make it easier to live with the most negative of behaviors.

Repetition, the Mother of Learning

First, ensure that the ground rules are well-defined and that the participants have consented to create, repeat and pledge to accept the ground rules. This will make it easier to deal with negative behaviors when they do occur. If the inappropriate behavior is covered in the ground rules, simply pointing it out will usually take care of it.

It's best to let the group point it out, even if you are the one to catch it. Simply ask the group: "Excuse me, but didn't we agree in our rules of conduct that we would not put anyone down for just asking a question?"

At this point, the group agrees and the person guilty of the infraction will usually apologize (or sulk off in silence) and the problem is solved, at least, for the moment.

Proximics

Second, remember your tools of proximics. If some participants are side-talking (carrying on a conversation apart from the group discussion and causing a distraction), simply moving closer to them may shut them down.

If need be, placing your hand on the table in front of them may be all it takes to make them aware of their behavior.

Going one step further, placing your hand on their backs without looking at them may do the trick.

Finally, all of the above PLUS looking at them with a smile, raising of the eyebrows or even a wink may be enough to get a person to conform to the group mandated norms.

Take it Off-Line

Third, if you spot a negative behavior but don't want to point it out at the meeting for political reasons (e.g., the behavior is from your boss) or to help the person save face, you may wish to take it off-line.

During a break or at lunch, counsel them about their behavior - they may not be aware that they are doing it.

Another off-line technique is to ask for their help as in: "I'm having trouble getting some members of the team to open up. Would you please be my partner and NOT share until I get two or three of the others to open up first? Then please share any new insights with the group. Otherwise, we'll not get the full value from this session. If I get stuck, I'll look over to you and give you a nod to help me kick off the discussion. Can I count on your help?"

Some might consider this devious or manipulative, but it is effective. On the occasions when we have used it, we really did mean it so it can be as sincere as it is effective.

Shut'em DOWN!

Fourth, swearing or overtly rude, sexist, racist, smutty, pornographic, prejudicial and other inappropriate comments should be shut down immediately and without regard for the person's feelings.

While some may argue against the validity of this approach, it is NEVER tolerated in any of our facilitations, seminars or workshops.

If you let one comment slide or if you take it off-line, you are giving tacit support for this sort of behavior and language. Is that the image you want to portray?

Best to nip it in the bud up front and not let it rear its ugly head again.

Sound of Silence

Fifth, silence is not golden in facilitation from the participants' standpoint and should not be tolerated. Ask the silent individual to share three points. Systematize™ if necessary.

Take them off-line and ask them why they are not participating or let them know how much you need their feedback.

Excuse them only if they are incapable of sharing because of a personal problem or some other legitimate reasons.

Silent "participants" in facilitation can become energy drains. In fact, they are not participants at all. Either people participate or they shouldn't be there. Facilitation is NOT a group lecture.

Deal with Dominators

Sixth, some folks want to dominate a discussion and will not give anyone else a chance. Groups with dominators tend to become monologues or dialog between the dominators while the rest of the group are reduced to being bystanders. Such participants rob the group of some really great ideas, diminishing the overall effectiveness.

To deal with dominators, consider these approaches:

1. Use proximics. Get closer to them if possible and stand next to them. This is intimidating and makes them feel a bit uncomfortable, often causing them to either realize they are talking too much or at the very least, limiting their input.

2. Say something along the lines of: "Thanks for that comment. Let's see if we can get input from at least three other people on this." This will at least give some others the chance to open up.

3. Go back to your ground rules and remind all of them (including the dominator) that ALL agreed to participate and that NO ONE can dominate the discussion.

   Of course, if this was not put into your ground rules in the beginning, it may be more difficult to add it later, but it should be possible to expand the ground rules with the group's buy-in.

4. Change the seating arrangement and put the dominator next to the person with the most power or authority. That sometimes quiets them down.

5. If the dominator IS the person with the most authority or power, go back to the ground rules and remind the entire group that all must contribute, etc.

   You can also take this person off-line at a break and remind them of the ground rules or say: "I really appreciate your input. I wish everyone in the group would contribute as much. I am having trouble getting some people to open up. Would you do me a favor and share half as much for the rest of the session? This would give me the opportunity to get some others to open up. If I STILL can't get them to open up, I'll give you a nod or ask you specifically to share and then you can add to what's already been said. Are you willing to help me out?"

6. If you have several dominators in a group of eight or more, break into smaller groups of up to six in a group. Put the dominators in ONE group and the others in another group or groups. Let

the dominators fight for "air time". The smaller group size will afford the more timid a less threatening, less competitive environment in which to be heard.

Find their Motivation

Seventh, if you are facilitating a hostile group that has been forced to attend, consider getting on their side. Ask them questions or state a purpose that shows you have empathy for their situation. "Trick" them into participating by giving them an incentive to get out of the meeting earlier.

For example, ask them, "How many of you would rather not be here?"

Follow this up with something like, "Me too. I've got so much work on my desk, you wouldn't believe it. Well, as we ARE here, we can either spend all day doing this or, if we can wrap it up by noon, we can get out of here and on our way. It's up to each of you. If we pull together and knock this off, then we can get out of here! If no one shares, it's gonna be a LONG day. Are you willing to help us get out of here faster?"

Emasculate the Intimidator

Eighth, if you have people who are intimidating participants because of their authority, physical size, display of wealth or knowledge, this can really inhibit input from the others and restrict the flow of information. You might have handled this up front in the ground rules, but if the problem persists, all is not lost.

Consider options like:

1. Asking them off-line to NOT be part of the group (only if this is appropriate and will not hurt the process).
2. Make the person an observer or scribe where they have mostly a non-speaking role. You can ask them questions at appropriate times to get them involved again.
3. Break the group into smaller groups and place the intimidator in a very small group of people with similar power positions if possible (MD with the VPs). The other groups will operate unhampered by this person's power.

4. If the problem is the perception of the team about this person's power and not the way that person is wielding the power, have that person share with the entire group that he or she is an equal in the group for this meeting. This relaxes some teams, although sometimes it doesn't have any effect. But the bottom line is – it rarely, if ever, *hurts* the process.

5. Use proximics with this person and assert your authority in the group over this person.

6. Review the ground rules stating that all are equal in the group for the accomplishment of the group's purpose.

7. Bring in someone of even greater power or authority who will not laud it over the team. This usually controls the power player whose behavior is "out of control".

chapter
11

Additional Thoughts

There is no one right way or style of facilitation and certainly, Mining For Gold™ is not perfect. We simply suggest that Mining For Gold™ is a way to strive for excellence, something that everyone is capable of attaining.

We can predict some people's objections to the overall process. Some might claim, "It's manipulative and not true facilitation."

No argument there from us.

In Mining For Gold™, we are attempting to help people discover their own answers. We are NOT about theory and ideas. It's about being practical and getting *results* – there are some of the key objections our detractors might have about Mining For Gold™.

Criticism #1

One main criticism is this – forcing answers and decisions in a short period of time instead of allowing "enough" time to the process.

Over the past 20 plus years, we found NO ONE, not ONE single company or organization that had unlimited amounts of time. ALL needed to get more done in less time. Just leaving people to their own devices turned out to be a huge waste of time and resources as well as being ineffective.

Getting good answers in a shorter period of time has turned out to be a boon for those who use our techniques.

Parkinson's law requires time limits and proves that our methods are effective. That is why our methodology sometimes flies in the face of "conventional wisdom".

"Common facilitation" in most instances assumes that the facilitator is truly neutral in the facilitation. He or she has no personal interest or hidden agenda and as such, will not take sides, get involved or be biased for or against the results.

But, this is like journalists reporting news instead of creating news. It NEVER happens. Take a political news story from another country. Read about it in that country's local paper. Then read about it in your own national paper. Then read about it in the International Herald Tribune. Finally, read about it in a financial paper like The Asian Wall Street Journal. You'll get four completely different views of the same story written by four different journalists, each of whom has pledged to uphold their neutrality.

The fact that human beings cannot be neutral is not a limitation, but an asset to be exploited. Use your best judgment to get the best results for your group.

If you have the best interests of the team at heart, do what you can to get the best results within the quickest possible time.

We believe neutrality is an ideal to strive for but in even the best cases involving a professional outside facilitator, that person can be biased towards the one who is the paymaster.

In the real world, everyone is biased and will manipulate agendas to get the results they prefer. In Mining For Gold™, we just start with the supposition up front that bias exists and then work towards minimizing its impact.

Perfection is also not going to come from the teams you are facilitating. Consider the case of the Asian manager we were told about by one of our program attendees. This guy had two marbles in his pocket; one red and one green. He kept these two marbles in his pocket to make his decisions.

When asked a question or when he had to make a decision, he would draw a marble from his pocket. If it was a red one, he would stop the project, not increase the budget or not hire the person. Whatever the question was, if he drew a red marble, the answer was "No!". If he produced a green marble, he'd go ahead with the idea, hire the person, increase the budget or proceed with the plan.

The attendee claimed his manager was right 80 percent of the time and was convinced it was fate, karma or some mystical power in the marbles.

As a student myself of Bayesian statistics, I assured him this was not the case. If you flip a coin, you always have a 50/50 chance of getting either a "heads" or a "tails". If you flipped the coin 1,000 times and always got "heads", the odds of it being a "heads" the next toss is STILL only 50 percent.

Likewise, the odds of producing a green or red marble out of the pocket (assuming they are of like size, shape, degree of smoothness and of uniform weight) is 50 percent.

The fact that the manager and perhaps everyone on his team believed in the "wisdom" of the marbles gave them a predisposition to work harder on projects that were "approved" by the "lucky" marbles.

In short, it didn't matter WHICH marble was drawn from the pocket. It was the follow-up, implementation and actions taken as a result of the draw that made these decisions "good decisions".

It was the follow-up that accounted for the 80 percent success rate. In fact, if the decisions had been based upon logic and reason, with the same kind of belief in the quality of the decision and the same enthusiastic follow-up, they might have found their decisions to be good 90 to 95 percent of the time.

The point is, a lot of facilitators are looking for perfect results from their teams, no matter how much time it takes to achieve it. They say things like, "To get quality decisions, you have to let the process take as much time as is needed."

Sorry folks, we totally disagree. What is needed most of the time in this fast changing world are quick, quality decisions that are followed up and acted upon immediately with enthusiasm, tenacity and due speed!

Criticism #2

Another criticism which we are leaving ourselves open for is, "If you are actively opening up some participants and shutting others down, you are manipulating the data and results, and that's not a facilitator's role."

To this we'll plead, "No contest." It is NOT the facilitator's role in the strictest sense of facilitation. The problem again is that very few of the millions of facilitations are pure facilitations. Most facilitators have a vested interest in the end result and can't help but be biased.

Criticism #3

Finally, some may criticize this book and the concept of Mining For Gold™ as overkill - too much ado about nothing. To this criticism, we also plead, "No contest." For most facilitations, you'll only need a part of this work. That's where you pick and choose what makes sense and what is overkill. The simpler and easier the facilitation, the less of this you'll need.

For some facilitations, however, even using ALL these techniques may not be enough. If that happens to you, it may be the perfect time to call in an external facilitator. Find someone with years of experience and a fresh, "outside-the-box" perspective. We hope this book is of benefit to you and your teams. With diligent planning and practice, you'll find that facilitation CAN be facilis or easy to do.

Mining For Gold™ is a great way of facilitating any meeting. We've been developing it since 1981 to be a quick turnkey method for gaining consensus, brainstorming, developing creative new ideas, coming up with team solutions and running daily meetings. Let a little Mining For Gold™ lead you to some incredibly valuable gold nuggets from your next facilitation or meeting!

Forms for
Mining For Gold™

"Here's the gold!"

Nothing is over until the paperwork is done. Mining For Gold™ is no exception. The paperwork for any facilitation takes several forms, including but not limited to:

1. The ripchart™ pages (flip chart pages) or notes taken along the way. These need to be summarized and recorded.

2. The report summary given to management or whoever called for the facilitation.

3. Your journal of facilitation notes of what went well with the process and what did not, so that you can learn and improve in future.
4. Your plan and process notes.
5. The SAFE Mining For Gold™ Checklist.
6. The Mining For Gold™ Facilitation Guide.
7. The Mining For Gold™ Checklist.

The following pages are set up for you to photocopys and use in your upcoming facilitations.

Form #1: Creating a SAFE Mining For Gold™ Environment

1. Prepare a SAFE environment in advance.

   - Can you Share something before you start?

   - Can you Affirm them and their efforts prior to the facilitation?

   - Is there a Fun way to introduce this facilitation to build up a little anticipation?

   - Can you show your Excitement prior to the facilitation?

   - Can you make it SAFE during the facilitation as well?

2. Know before you go.

   - Who can help you?

   - Hurt you?

   - Hurt someone else?

   - Sabotage the effort?

© 2004 Podolinsky International Pte Ltd

Form #1: Creating a SAFE Mining For Gold™ Environment (continued)

3. Who do you need to protect?

4. How will you protect them?

5. Before you start, list methods of encouragement you will use.

6. At the start of the facilitation, explain the ground rules, your role, their role, the goal and time constraints.

7. As issues arise, be prepared to talk to the offending parties on- or off-line.

Form #2: Mining For Gold™ Checklist

1. Is everyone who needs to be there attending? ☐
2. Have I formulated a plan to ensure success, including ground rules and a method of buy-in? ☐
3. Do I know everything about the participants, such as their hidden agendas, what they might want to accomplish, their comfort level in speaking, willingness to share and trust level? ☐
4. Am I excited and showing an appropriate level of energy? ☐
5. What exercises am I planning to bring out more participation? ☐
6. Who will be my co-facilitators and why? How can we best work together? ☐
7. Does everyone know in advance what to bring, why he or she is coming and what to expect? ☐
8. How am I ensuring timeliness of this facilitation? ☐
9. Am I encouraging without appearing artificial? ☐
10. Am I keeping everyone on track without cutting anyone off? ☐
11. What am I doing to both reward and encourage participation? ☐
12. What rewards am I using? ☐
13. How am I ensuring follow-up by ALL involved? ☐
14. Is my dress and appearance appropriate to open them up? ☐
15. Do I let my personal opinions dominate or am I open to the group's input? ☐
16. How do I ensure that the group gets rewarded for their efforts AFTER the meeting? ☐
17. Do I have the authority or did I get the authority for the group from management so that they can implement whatever they decide? If not, does the group know the limitations of their power and expectations? ☐
18. Are everyone else and I having FUN? ☐

© 2004 Podolinsky International Pte Ltd

Form #3: Mining For Gold™ Facilitation Guide

Pre-meeting Analysis

1. What kind of a meeting is this?

2. What is the purpose of this meeting?

3. What outcome do I hope to accomplish?

4. Who needs to be there?

5. Who will attend?

6. Who will help us achieve our desired goal?

© 2004 Podolinsky International Pte Ltd

Pre-meeting Analysis (continued)

7. Who will detract from this meeting? How?

8. How can I prevent this problem BEFORE it starts?

9. How can I minimize any negative influence during the process?

10. How can I minimize its impact after the process?

11. What is the best way to get each attendee to open up?

12. What do I need to do to get them to TRUST me?

13. How can I "salt" the group to help me?

During the Meeting

1. Ground rules used:
   - My role:

   - Their role:

   - The goal:

   - Time limits:

2. NLP modes used:
   Auditory/Visual kinesthetic

3. Consensus tools used:
   Result:

4. Communications checklist:

   - Proactive listening ☐

   - Dynamic directions ☐

   - Proactive observation ☐

   - Proactive feedback ☐

   - Proactive encouragement ☐

During the Meeting (continued)

- Proactive coaching ☐

- Proactive summarization ☐

5. In dealing with difficult types, have I been:
   - Friendly? ☐

   - Honest? ☐

   - Fair? ☐

   - Fun? ☐

   - Functional? ☐

   - Firm? ☐

   - Direct? ☐

6. Describe how the process went in general:

7. Who helped the process flow:

8. Who hindered the process:

Post Meeting Analysis

Group's reaction (their evaluation):

1	2	3	4	5	6	7	8	9	10
poor		fine			good	very good			excellent

Results achieved:

1	2	3	4	5	6	7	8	9	10
poor		fine			good	very good			excellent

My reaction:

1	2	3	4	5	6	7	8	9	10
poor		fine			good	very good			excellent

Reaction of those in charge (attending or not):

1	2	3	4	5	6	7	8	9	10
poor		fine			good	very good			excellent

Changes I'll make for next time:

Additional comments:

These forms may not cover all the bases but are a good start to Mining For Gold™. Feel free to add to them as the need arises. We'd also appreciate any suggestions you might have for these forms or this book. In subsequent editions and in our newsletter, we'll acknowledge your contributions and might just send you a free gift for the contribution.

Resource and Bibliography

Resource

International Association of Facilitators, The, www.iaf-world.org
14985 Glazier Avenue Suite 550 St. Paul MN 55124 USA
Tel: 952-891-3541; Fax: 952-891-1800; Email: OFFICE@iaf-world.org

Bibliography

Cameron, Ester. *Facilitation Made Easy: Practical Tips to Improve Facilitation Techniques*. Kogan Page Ltd, 1998.

Charles, Leslie and Chris Clarke-Epstein. *The Instant Trainer*. McGraw-Hill, 1997.

Friedberger, Julie. *Office Yoga: Tackling Tension with Simple Stretches You can Do at Your Desk*. Motilal Banarsidass Publishers, 2000.

Hackett, Donald and Charles L. Martin. *Facilitation Skills for Team Leaders*. Crisp Publications, Inc., 1993.

Hunter, Dale, Anne Bailey and Bill Taylor. *The Art of Facilitation: How to Create Group Synergy*. Perseus Publishing, 1995.

Hunter, Dale, Anne Bailey and Bill Taylor. *Zen of Groups: A Handbook for People Meeting With a Purpose*. Perseus Publishing, 1995.

Justice, Thomas and David Jamieson. *The Facilitator's Fieldbook: Step by Step Procedures, Checklists and Guidelines, Samples and Templates*. AMACOM, 1999.

Learning Emporium, The, "Your One Stop Training Shop™", www.learningemporium.com.

Percy, Ian. *Going Deep: Exploring Spirituality in Life and Leadership*. Inspired Productions Press, 2002.

Pike, Bob (ed). *Creative Training Techniques Newsletter*. Vnu Inc.

Putz, Gregory B. *Facilitation Skills: Helping Groups Make Decisions*. Deep Space Technology Company, 2002.

Ray, Glenn. *The Facilitative Leader: Behaviors That Enable Success.* Prentice Hall, 1998.

Rees, Fran and Matt Holt. *Facilitator Excellence Handbook: Helping People Work Creatively and Productively Together.* Jossey-Bass Publishers, Inc. Pfeiffer, 1998.

Rees, Fran. *How to Lead Work Teams: Facilitation Skills.* Jossey-Bass Publishers, Inc. Pfeiffer, 2001.

Reitz, Helen L. and Marilyn Manning. *The One Stop Guide to Workshops.* McGraw-Hill, 1993.

Scannell, Edward E., John W. Newstrom and Carolyn D. Nilson. *Games Trainers Play.* McGraw-Hill, 1980.

Scannell, Edward E. and John W. Newstrom. *More Games Trainers Play.* McGraw-Hill, 1983.

Scannell, Edward E. and John W. Newstrom. *Still More Games Trainers Play.* McGraw-Hill, 1991.

Scannell, Edward E. and John W. Newstrom. *Even More Games Trainers Play.* McGraw-Hill, 1994.

Silberman, Mel and Karen Lawson. *101 Ways to Make Training More Active.* Jossey-Bass Pfeiffer, 1995.

Williams, Linda. *Teaching for the Two Sided Mind: A Guide To Right Brain/Left Brain Education.* Touchstone Books, 1986.

Zemke, Ron (ed). *Training (magazine).* Reed Business Information Ltd.

Facilitation and Training Supplies

Creative Learning Tools (USA), www.CreativeLearningTools.com
Oriental Trading Company (USA) (giveaways), www.oriental.com
Check your local yellow pages under wholesale confectionery, wholesale toys and wholesale incentives.

About the Author

Michael A. Podolinsky is a world-class facilitator. Having conducted over 1,700 facilitations, training program, seminars and speeches, he has developed an easy to understand and use methodology that anyone can apply.

Facilitating on six continents in 23 countries for more than 500 clients, Podolinsky developed Mining For Gold™ since 1981 as a groundbreaking and definitive work on facilitation. He totally disagrees with the pack who insists, "Let it take as long as it takes to get quality answers from your team." Those who practice Mining For Gold™ are able to get more done in less time through what he calls a "creative pressure cooker".

The only twice past president of the prestigious National Speakers Association - Minnesota Chapter, one of five Americans named "Honorary Member of the National Speakers Association of Australia", a founding member of the Asia Speakers Association and named "Consummate Speaker of the Year" by Walter's International Speakers Bureau, Podolinsky has the platform skills as well as the real-world practical experience to make facilitations not just fun, but effective.

Based in Singapore since 2003, his business has been serving Australia, New Zealand and Asia since 1987. From Mongolia to Dunedin, Hong Kong to Perth, Bangkok to Manila, Podolinsky and his business, Podolinsky International Pte Ltd, have developed a 90 percent repeat or referral reputation.

To have a program conducted within your organization, you can contact Michael at:

Podolinsky International Pte Ltd
6 Petir Road, #05-06
Singapore 678267
Phone: (65) 6764-8067
For more information, you may check out his web site at:
www.michaelpodolinsky.com
or e-mail him at: mike@michaelpodolinsky.com

Podolinsky's public seminars in Singapore are conducted through the Singapore Institute of Management and those interested can contact the Public Seminars Division at

Phone: (65) 6468-8866

Additional Programs and Training Options

In addition to this book, we offer one-on-one coaching in Mining For Gold™, Presentamagic™ (presentation skills), creative training skills, management, leadership and time management skills. For groups, we conduct the following courses:

- "Mining For Gold™... Facilitation Skills for Managers, Trainers and Team Leaders"
- "Managerial Magic™... How to Manage, Motivate and Maintain a High Profit, High Productivity Team"

  The essentials of motivation, leadership, delegation, management, communications, team-building and problem-solving.
- "Tick Talk™... How to DOUBLE Your Productivity and TRIPLE Your Effectiveness Through Proactive Time and Stress Management"

  From goal-setting and life-planning to balancing life with the 5 "F's", this course covers all the keys for controlling interruptions, advancing your career and getting more out of your work and life.
- "How to Become a More Creative and Effective Trainer, Teacher or Presenter"

  Teaching trainers and those who conduct meetings and trainings how to use magic, props, ice-breakers, group activities to make training more fun and effective. Also, we teach how to turn training into games and how adults learn best.
- "Presentamagic™... How to Easily Deliver an Effective Presentation EVERY Time You Speak"

  Teaching a fun and easy system for how to deliver highly effective presentations with zest.
- "Montai Magic... The Professional's Secret Weapon!"

  A fun and entertaining motivational keynote speech teaching six disciplines for success and how to overcome our barriers.

- Custom made presentations geared around developing people.
- "Sell More, Sell Smarter™... A Comprehensive Sales Training and Motivational Program"

   Teaching saleperson how to prospect, creat a positive impression, build rapport, read a prospect using NLP, handle objections, build long-term relationships, stay motivated and CLOSE that sale!